QUÉBEC

POCKET TRAVEL GUIDE

Travel smarter, not harder,

with this insider's guide.

John Stone C.

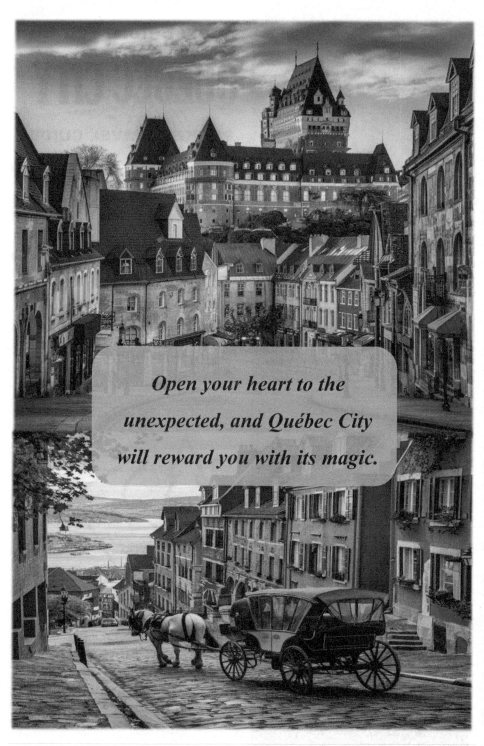

Open your heart to the unexpected, and Québec City will reward you with its magic.

Disclaimer:

While we have diligently strived for accuracy in this guide, please note that details like prices, hours, and contact information may change. We encourage you to confirm these details with official sources before your trip.

TABLE OF CONTENTS

INTRODUCTION...8

1. WELCOME TO QUÉBEC CITY!...13

A Glimpse of European Charm 13

Why Québec City is Special 14

Geography (A Brief Overview) 15

Fun Facts & Hidden Facts: 16

2. BEFORE YOU GO..22

Things You Should Know When Traveling to Québec 22

Visas & Essentials 24

Money Matters...26

Travel Budget Planner (Estimating Costs).....................28

Best Time to Travel (Seasonal Highlights & Considerations) 31

What to Pack (Including Seasonal Advice)....................33

3. GETTING AROUND..38

Arriving & Departing: Your Gateway to Québec City........38

City Transportation...41

Handy Map..44

4. QUÉBEC CITY WITH KIDS..46

Family-Friendly Attractions: Family Fun in a Charming Setting 46

Kid-Approved Activities..48

Tips for Traveling with Children 50

5. MUST-SEE SIGHTS..54

Iconic Landmarks: Québec City's Crown Jewels 54

Charming Neighborhoods: Québec City's Hidden Treasure 58

Cultural Hotspots 60

Natural Escapes 63

6. OFF-THE-BEATEN-PATH..67

Hidden Gems & Local Secrets 67

Unique Experiences..68

7. LOCAL FLAVORS 71

Must-Try Dishes: A Taste of Québec............................71

Traditional Restaurants 75

Markets & Shops: Where to Shop & What to Shop.........77

Cafés & Restaurants 80

8. QUÉBEC CITY AFTER DARK 84

Bars & Pubs for Every Taste......................................84

Live Music & Entertainment: 86

Festivals & Events 88

9. DAY TRIPS & EXCURSIONS 92

Île d'Orléans 92

Montmorency Falls Park 94

Wendake Huron Village..97

10. ACCOMMODATIONS...100

11. ACTIVITIES & EXPERIENCES 114

Outdoor Adventures: Get Active in Québec City 114

Experiencing Local Culture (Museums, Art Galleries, Shows
....116

Family Fun (Parks, Zoos, Playgrounds) 118

Seasonal Activities (Winter Carnivals, Summer Festivals)
....122

12. PRACTICAL TIPS..126

Local Customs & Etiquette 126

Useful French Phrases 128

Things to Avoid (Common Tourist Traps or Mistakes) 132

Staying Safe & Connected (Emergency Contacts)......... 136

Languages Spoken in Québec..................................... 138

Suggested Itinenary 140

CONCLUSION..143

Word Search Fun 144

- **Before You Go:**

  - ❖ Browse the guide to get acquainted with Québec City.

  - ❖ Use the Travel Budget Planner to estimate costs.

  - ❖ Choose attractions and activities that pique your interest.

  - ❖ Craft your itinerary using our suggestions or personalize it!

- **While You're There:**

  - ❖ Carry the guide with you for easy reference.

  - ❖ Check the "Practical Tips" for cultural insights and safety info.

  - ❖ Embrace spontaneity and explore beyond the planned itinerary.

  - ❖ Most importantly, have fun and enjoy your Québec City adventure!

Bonus Tips:

- Highlight or mark your favorite spots.

- Jot down your own notes and memories.

"Bonjour, eh? Practice your French, but don't worry about perfection. A smile and a 'merci' will go a long way."

INTRODUCTION

Québec City, a city of striking contrasts, seamlessly blends European elegance with North American spirit. Steeped in history yet vibrantly modern, this UNESCO World Heritage treasure boasts cobblestone streets that echo with tales of explorers and settlers, while its bustling markets and lively festivals pulse with the rhythm of contemporary life. Whether you're fascinated by the scenic beauty of the St. Lawrence River, drawn to the layers of its rich history, or eager to savor the culinary delights that excite your taste buds, Québec City offers an experience that is truly unique.

Yet, navigating this enchanting city can be overwhelming, especially for first-time visitors. That's why we created this Pocket Travel Guide, your trusted companion on your Québec City adventure.

What Makes This Guide Special:

- **Comprehensive:** We've meticulously gathered all the essential information you'll need to plan and enjoy your trip, from the city's history and cultural nuances to practical tips on getting around and staying safe.

- **Accommodations Expertise:** We've handpicked a diverse selection of accommodations, ranging from budget-friendly hostels and charming bed and breakfasts to luxurious boutique hotels, each with detailed contact information (phone numbers and addresses) to simplify your booking process.

- **Easy to Use:** This guide is designed with you in mind. The clear and concise information is organized in a way that's easy to navigate, so you can quickly find what you need, whether you're on the go or relaxing in your hotel room.

- **Insightful:** We've gone beyond the surface-level details to offer valuable insights and recommendations based on personal experiences and extensive research. You'll discover hidden gems, local favorites, and unique experiences that you won't find in typical guidebooks.

- **Pocket-Sized:** This compact guide is designed to fit easily in your pocket or bag, making it your constant companion as you explore the city.

- **Interactive & Fun:** We've included engaging features like sample itineraries, and even word search puzzles to enhance your experience and make planning your trip a breeze.

- And a lot more to be discovered within the book.

No matter if you're a history buff, a foodie, an outdoor enthusiast, or simply seeking a charming escape, this Pocket Travel Guide is your key to revealing the magic of Québec City. Pack your bags, lace up your walking shoes, and get ready to engage yourself in the timeless charm and interesting culture of this extraordinary city. Your Québec City adventure awaits!

1. WELCOME TO QUÉBEC CITY!

A Glimpse of European Charm

Bonjour and welcome to Québec City, a jewel of North America that sparkles with European charm! As you step onto the cobblestone streets of Old Québec, a UNESCO World Heritage treasure, you'll feel like you've traveled back in time to a quaint French village. The air is filled with the sweet scent of fresh croissants from local bakeries, and the sound of church bells ringing echoes through the narrow lanes.

But don't be fooled – Québec City is far from stuck in the past. This vibrant city seamlessly blends old-world traditions with modern energy. Cutting-edge museums and art galleries showcase contemporary talent, while trendy boutiques and bustling markets offer a glimpse into the city's creative spirit.

As you wander through the charming neighborhoods, you'll be captivated by the colorful houses, wrought-iron balconies, and grand cathedrals that dot the landscape. And no matter where you are, the majestic St. Lawrence River is never far away, offering stunning views and a refreshing breeze. Whether you're exploring the historic fortifications, strolling along the bustling streets, or simply soaking up the ambiance, Québec City is sure to charm you with its unique blend of old and new.

Why Québec City is Special

Québec City isn't just another charming city; it's a living testament to history and culture, recognized as a UNESCO World Heritage site. Imagine walking through a real-life postcard of 17th and 18th-century architecture, with cobblestone streets echoing tales of French explorers and settlers. That's Old Québec, the heart of the city, where you'll find the majestic Château Frontenac, the imposing Citadelle, and the charming Place Royale – all reminders of Québec's rich past.

But Québec City isn't just about history. It's a cultural powerhouse, buzzing with energy and creativity. World-class museums like the Musée de la Civilisation showcase the city's unique heritage, while cutting-edge art galleries like the Musée national des beaux-arts du Québec display contemporary works that inspire and provoke.

And let's not forget the festivals! From the world-renowned Winter Carnival, a frosty wonderland of ice sculptures and snow slides, to the vibrant Summer Festival, filled with music, dance, and street performers, Québec City knows how to celebrate.

Foodies, rejoice! Québec City's culinary scene is a delicious blend of French and Canadian influences. Savor mouthwatering poutine (fries, cheese curds, and gravy), indulge in rich tourtière (meat pie), and try tarte flambée, a thin-crust pizza-like dish. And don't forget to sample the local maple syrup – it's simply the best!

Québec City is more than just a pretty face. It's a city with a soul, where history, culture, and creativity come together to create an experience you won't find anywhere else.

Geography (A Brief Overview)

Québec City is perched dramatically on the northern banks of the mighty St. Lawrence River, in the heart of the province of Québec, Canada. The city is divided into two distinct areas: Upper Town and Lower Town.

Upper Town (Haute-Ville): Sitting atop a cliff overlooking the river, Upper Town is where you'll find most of the city's historic landmarks, including the imposing Château Frontenac and the star-shaped Citadelle. This area is known for its charming cobblestone streets, grand architecture, and panoramic views.

Lower Town (Basse-Ville): Nestled at the foot of the cliff, Lower Town exudes a more intimate and lively atmosphere. It's home to Place Royale, the birthplace of Québec City, as well as charming shops, cafes, and restaurants lining the narrow streets.

Beyond the city walls, Québec City is surrounded by picturesque landscapes. To the north, the Laurentian Mountains offer opportunities for hiking, skiing, and exploring nature. To the east, the tranquil Île d'Orléans (Island of Orléans) beckons with its orchards, farms, and charming villages. Whether you're exploring the city or venturing into the surrounding countryside, you'll be captivated by Québec City's unique setting and natural beauty.

Fun Facts & Hidden Facts:

- Did you know that Québec City is the only remaining fortified city in North America north of Mexico? Its 4.6 kilometers of walls, gates, and towers transport you back to the 17th and 18th centuries.

- The Château Frontenac holds the Guinness World Record for the most photographed hotel in the world! Its fairytale-like appearance and prominent location make it an irresistible subject for photographers.

- Forget Paris – Québec City is the snowshoe capital of the world! With its snowy winters and stunning scenery, it's no wonder this unique sport is so popular here.

- Québec City loves its staircases! In fact, there are nearly 30 public stairways scattered throughout the city, connecting different neighborhoods and offering breathtaking views. Be prepared to get those steps in!

- Québec City is home to a real-life ice hotel, Hôtel de Glace, constructed entirely of snow and ice each winter. It's a magical place where you can sleep in a sub-zero room, sip cocktails in ice glasses, and even get married in an ice chapel!

- Foodies, rejoice! Poutine, the iconic Canadian dish of fries, cheese curds, and gravy, was actually invented in Québec in the 1950s. Prepare to indulge in this local delicacy at one of the many "poutineries" across the city.

- Québec City may be known for its French heritage, but it also has a strong Irish influence. You'll find several Irish pubs and even a St. Patrick's Day parade in the city!

- Looking for a unique experience? You can spend the night in a former monastery, now the beautiful Le Monastère des Augustines hotel. It's a tranquil retreat in the heart of Old Québec.

- Art lovers will be delighted by the city's vibrant street art scene. Keep an eye out for colorful murals and creative installations as you wander through the streets.

- If you're visiting during winter, don't miss the chance to skate on Place D'Youville, an outdoor rink with stunning views of the city walls. It's a truly magical experience!

Historical Tidbits:

- Québec City's nickname is "the Gibraltar of the Americas" due to its strategic location atop a cliff and its imposing fortifications.

- The city's iconic Château Frontenac was named after Louis de Buade, Comte de Frontenac, who served as Governor of New France twice in the 17th century.

- Place Royale, the heart of Old Québec, was once a bustling marketplace where Indigenous people and French settlers traded furs and goods.

- The Plains of Abraham, a historic battlefield, is now a peaceful park where locals and visitors enjoy picnics, cycling, and stunning views of the St. Lawrence River.

Cultural Curiosities:

- Québec City is home to the oldest French-language university in North America, Université Laval, founded in 1663.

- The city boasts a vibrant arts scene, with numerous galleries, theaters, and music venues showcasing local and international talent.

- The Musée de la Civilisation is one of Canada's most popular museums, offering interactive exhibits on Québec's history, culture, and society.

- Québec City's annual Winter Carnival is one of the largest winter festivals in the world, attracting visitors from around the globe with its ice sculptures, snow slides, and festive atmosphere.

Local Legends and Lore:

- The ghost of a young woman named Lady in White is said to haunt the Plains of Abraham, searching for her lost love.

- The Petit Champlain district is rumored to be home to friendly ghosts who roam the streets at night.

- Legend has it that a secret tunnel connects the Château Frontenac to the Citadelle, although its existence has never been confirmed.

Offbeat Attractions:

- The Morrin Centre, a former prison turned cultural center, offers a fascinating glimpse into Québec City's past.

- The Observatoire de la Capitale, located on the 31st floor of the Marie-Guyart Building, provides panoramic views of the city and surrounding landscapes.

- The Quartier Saint-Sauveur, a working-class neighborhood, is known for its authentic character, local shops, and lively atmosphere.

Quirky Facts:

- Québec City has a love affair with staircases! With nearly 30 public stairways scattered throughout the city, you're sure to get a good workout while exploring.

- The city is home to the only ice hotel in North America, Hôtel de Glace, a magical winter wonderland made entirely of snow and ice.

- Québec City's official motto is "Je me souviens" (I remember), a reminder of its rich history and cultural heritage.

With these fun facts and hidden gems in mind, your Québec City adventure is sure to be filled with surprises and unforgettable moments!

2. BEFORE YOU GO

Things You Should Know When Traveling to Québec

Cultural Nuances:

Québec City has a rich cultural heritage and a strong sense of politeness. When interacting with locals, remember to be courteous and respectful. A simple "bonjour" (hello) or "bonsoir" (good evening) goes a long way in showing appreciation for their culture. You'll often hear "merci" (thank you) in response, so be sure to reciprocate.

In Québec, personal space is valued, so avoid standing too close to people or touching them unnecessarily. When in doubt, observe how locals interact and follow their lead.

Currency & Tipping:

Québec City uses the Canadian dollar (CAD) as its currency. You can easily exchange your currency at banks, exchange bureaus, or hotels. Credit cards are widely accepted, but it's a good idea to carry some cash for smaller purchases or in case you encounter places that don't accept cards.

Tipping is customary in Québec City, especially in restaurants, bars, and hotels. For good service, a tip of 15-20% is expected in restaurants and bars. In hotels, you can tip the bellhop $2-5 CAD per bag and the housekeeper $2-5 CAD per night.

Language Considerations:

While French is the official language of Québec, English is widely spoken and understood in tourist areas and by most people working in the hospitality industry. However, making an effort to speak a few basic French phrases will be greatly appreciated by locals.

Below are some helpful phrases to begin with:

- Bonjour (Hello)
- Bonsoir (Good evening/night)
- Au revoir (Goodbye)
- Merci (Thank you)

- S'il vous plaît (Please)

- Excusez-moi (Excuse me)

- Parlez-vous anglais? (Do you speak English?)

- Je ne comprends pas (I don't understand)

- See more on page 128.

Don't be afraid to try your hand at French, even if you're not fluent. Locals are generally patient and understanding, and your effort will go a long way in making a positive impression.

By keeping these cultural nuances, currency tips, and language considerations in mind, you'll be well-prepared to enjoy a smooth and respectful trip to Québec City!

Visas & Essentials

Before beginning your Québec City adventure, it's essential to ensure you have all the necessary travel documents.

Visa Requirements:

Most international travelers, including those from the United States, the United Kingdom, Australia, and many European countries, do not need a visa for stays of up to six months in Canada. However, it's always wise to double-check the specific requirements for your country of origin on the official Government of Canada website.

If you do need a visa, you'll typically need to apply well in advance of your trip and provide documentation such as a valid passport, proof of funds, and a detailed itinerary.

Electronic Travel Authorization (eTA):

Even if you don't need a visa, some travelers may require an Electronic Travel Authorization (eTA) to fly to or transit through Canada. This applies to citizens of certain visa-exempt countries who arrive by air. You can apply for an eTA online through the Government of Canada website. It's a simple process and usually takes just a few minutes.

Travel Insurance:

While not mandatory, it's highly recommended to purchase travel insurance before your trip. This will protect you in case of unexpected events like flight cancellations, medical emergencies, or lost luggage.

Vaccinations and Health Precautions:

There are no mandatory vaccinations to enter Canada. However, it is recommended to keep your routine vaccinations updated. Depending on your planned activities and the time of year you visit, you might consider packing insect repellent and sunscreen.

I hope this information helps you prepare for a smooth and enjoyable trip to Québec City!

Money Matters

As stated earlier, Québec City uses the Canadian dollar (CAD) as its currency. You'll find it easy to manage your money during your visit, as the city offers various convenient options:

Currency Exchange:

If you're arriving with foreign currency, you have a few options for exchanging it into Canadian dollars:

- **Currency Exchange Bureaus:** You'll find these at the airport, train station, and in some hotels and tourist areas. Be sure to compare rates and fees between different bureaus to get the best deal.

- **Banks:** Most banks in Québec City offer currency exchange services, typically with lower fees than exchange bureaus. Your passport may be required as proof of identity.

- **ATMs:** The easiest and often most cost-effective way to get Canadian dollars is by withdrawing them directly from an ATM using your debit or credit card. ATMs are widely available throughout the city. However, be aware that your bank might charge foreign transaction fees, so check with them beforehand.

Credit Cards & Mobile Payments:

Credit cards are widely accepted in Québec City, including major ones like Visa, Mastercard, and American Express. You can use them for most purchases, from hotel stays and restaurant bills to souvenirs and museum tickets.

Mobile payment options like Apple Pay and Google Pay are also becoming increasingly popular, especially in larger establishments. However, carrying some cash is always a good idea for smaller shops, markets, or tipping.

Tips:

- Before your trip, notify your bank or credit card company that you'll be traveling to Québec City to avoid any issues with your cards being blocked for security reasons.

- Consider getting a credit card with no foreign transaction fees to save on extra charges.

- Download a currency conversion app on your phone to easily calculate prices and track your spending.

By understanding the currency exchange process and payment options available in Québec City, you'll be well-equipped to manage your finances and enjoy your trip to the fullest!

Travel Budget Planner (Estimating Costs)

Planning your budget is key to enjoying your trip without breaking the bank. Below is an estimated breakdown of costs you can expect in Québec City, along with some savvy tips for stretching your dollars:

Accommodation:

- **Budget:** Hostels and budget hotels: $25-$50 USD per night

- **Mid-Range:** Comfortable hotels and guesthouses: $75-$150 USD per night

- **Luxury:** Boutique hotels and historic inns: $150-$300+ USD per night

Budget-Friendly Tip: Consider staying in a hostel, Airbnb, or guesthouse outside of the Old Town. You'll often find more affordable options while still being within easy reach of the city center by public transportation. Look for special offers and discounts during the shoulder seasons (spring and fall).

Meals:

- **Breakfast:** Pastries from local bakeries or cafes: $5-$10 USD

- **Lunch:** Sandwiches, salads, or poutine from casual eateries: $10-$20 USD

- **Dinner:** Mid-range restaurants: $20-$40 USD per person; Upscale dining: $50+ USD per person

Budget-Friendly Tip: Embrace Québec's street food scene! Sample local delicacies like poutine or tourtière from food trucks and stalls for a fraction of the price of a sit-down meal. Look for "table d'hôte" menus, which offer a multi-course meal at a fixed price. Picnic in one of the city's parks with local cheeses, bread, and fruits from a grocery store.

Transportation:

- **Bus Fare (RTC):** Single ticket: $3.50 CAD (approx. $2.60 USD); Day pass: $8.50 CAD (approx. $6.30 USD)

- **Taxi:** Starting fare around $3.50 CAD (approx. $2.60 USD), plus metered rate

- **Bike Rental:** $10-$20 USD per day

Budget-Friendly Tip: Invest in a multi-day bus pass if you plan on using public transportation frequently. Québec City is also very walkable, especially in the Old Town, so consider exploring on foot to save on transportation costs.

Activities:

- **Free Attractions:** Explore the Plains of Abraham, stroll through the historic Old Town, admire the street art in Saint-Roch, or visit free museums on certain days.

- **Discounted Activities:** Many museums and attractions offer reduced rates for students, seniors, or families. Look for combo tickets or city passes for additional savings.

Overall Budget:

- **Budget Traveler:** $50-$75 USD per day (hostels, street food, public transportation, free activities)

- **Mid-Range Traveler:** $100-$150 USD per day (comfortable hotels, dining out occasionally, some paid activities)

- **Luxury Traveler:** $200+ USD per day (upscale accommodations, fine dining, guided tours, splurge activities)

Remember, these are just estimates. Your individual spending will depend on your travel style and choices. By planning and budgeting wisely, you can make the most of your Québec City experience without overspending!

Best Time to Travel (Seasonal Highlights & Considerations)

Québec City is a year-round destination, each season offering a unique experience:

Summer (June-August):

- **Appeal:** Warm and sunny days perfect for outdoor activities, festivals, and patio dining.

- **Highlights:** Festival d'été de Québec (July), New France Festival (August), and outdoor concerts in the Plains of Abraham.

- **Weather:** Temperatures average 20-25°C (68-77°F) with occasional heatwaves.

- **What to Pack:** Light clothing, shorts, t-shirts, sunglasses, sunscreen, and a hat.

Fall (September-October):

- **Appeal:** Vibrant fall foliage, crisp air, and fewer crowds.

- **Highlights:** The changing colors of the leaves in the surrounding parks and countryside.

- **Weather:** Temperatures range from 10-20°C (50-68°F) with cool evenings.

- **What to Pack:** Layers (sweaters, jackets), long pants, comfortable walking shoes, and a light scarf or hat.

Winter (November-March):

- **Appeal:** Winter wonderland atmosphere, Québec Winter Carnival (February), outdoor winter sports (skiing, snowboarding, snowshoeing).

- **Highlights:** Hôtel de Glace (Ice Hotel), German Christmas Market, and Toboggan Slide Au 1884.

- **Weather:** Cold and snowy, with temperatures often below freezing (-5 to -15°C or 23-5°F).

- **What to Pack:** Warm layers (thermal underwear, sweaters, fleece jacket), waterproof winter coat, snow pants, warm boots, gloves, hat, scarf.

Spring (April-May):

- **Appeal:** Mild temperatures, blooming flowers, and fewer tourists than summer.

- **Highlights:** Maple syrup season (sugar shacks are open for traditional meals), and the city begins to awaken after the winter slumber.

- **Weather:** Temperatures range from 5-15°C (41-59°F) with occasional rain.

- **What to Pack:** Layers (sweaters, light jackets), waterproof shoes, and an umbrella.

No matter when you visit, Québec City offers something special. Select the time of year that aligns with your interests and desires!

Remember, this is just a general guideline. For the most up-to-date weather information, be sure to check the forecast closer to your travel dates.

What to Pack (Including Seasonal Advice)

Spring (April-May):

- **Clothing:**
  - ✓ Light to medium-weight layers (t-shirts, long-sleeved shirts, sweaters)

- ✓ Light jacket or raincoat

- ✓ Jeans or comfortable pants

- ✓ Comfortable walking shoes or sneakers

- ✓ Umbrella or waterproof jacket (for unpredictable spring showers)

- **Footwear:**

  - ✓ Waterproof shoes or boots (for occasional rain)

  - ✓ Comfortable walking shoes for exploring the city

- **Other Essentials:**

  - ✓ Sunglasses

  - ✓ Sunscreen

  - ✓ Hat

  - ✓ Insect repellent (if spending time outdoors)

Summer (June-August):

- **Clothing:**

  - ✓ Light and breathable clothing (shorts, t-shirts, sundresses)

  - ✓ Light sweater or jacket for cooler evenings

  - ✓ Comfortable walking shoes or sandals

✓ Swimwear (if visiting beaches or pools)

- **Footwear:**

  ✓ Sandals or flip-flops for warm weather

  ✓ Comfortable walking shoes for exploring the city

- **Other Essentials:**

  ✓ Sunglasses

  ✓ Sunscreen

  ✓ Hat

  ✓ Insect repellent

Fall (September-October):

- **Clothing:**

  ✓ Layers (t-shirts, long-sleeved shirts, sweaters, light jacket)

  ✓ Raincoat or waterproof jacket

  ✓ Jeans or comfortable pants

  ✓ Comfortable walking shoes or boots

  ✓ Scarf and gloves (for chilly days and nights)

- **Footwear:**

  ✓ Waterproof shoes or boots

✓ Comfortable walking shoes

- **Other Essentials:**

  ✓ Umbrella

Winter (November-March):

- **Clothing:**

  ✓ Warm layers (thermal underwear, sweaters, fleece jacket)

  ✓ Waterproof and insulated winter coat

  ✓ Snow pants or waterproof pants

  ✓ Warm socks (wool or synthetic)

  ✓ Hat, scarf, and gloves or mittens

- **Footwear:**

  ✓ Insulated, waterproof winter boots with good traction

- **Other Essentials:**

  ✓ Sunglasses (the sun reflecting off the snow can be bright)

  ✓ Hand and foot warmers (optional)

Additional Items for Specific Activities:

- **Hiking:** Hiking boots, backpack, water bottle, snacks

- **Biking:** Helmet, bike gloves, padded shorts (if biking for longer periods)

- **Kayaking:** Waterproof jacket and pants, hat, sunscreen, sunglasses, water shoes

General Packing Tips:

- Don't forget to bring any required medications, toiletries, and personal belongings.

- Pack a universal adapter if your electronic devices have a different plug type than the ones used in your destination.

- Consider packing a small first-aid kit.

- Check the weather forecast before you go and adjust your packing accordingly.

3. GETTING AROUND

Arriving & Departing: Your Gateway to Québec City

Québec City is easily accessible by various modes of transportation, making it a convenient destination for travelers:

By Plane:

- Jean Lesage International Airport (YQB): Located just 16 km (10 miles) from downtown Québec City, YQB offers direct flights from major Canadian cities (Toronto, Montreal, etc.), select U.S. cities (New York, Chicago), and some European destinations.

- Navigating YQB: The airport is relatively small and easy to navigate. After collecting your luggage, you'll find several transportation options in the arrivals area, including taxis, rental cars, and public buses. There are also luggage storage facilities available if you need to store your bags before heading to your accommodation.

By Train:

- VIA Rail: Québec City's Gare du Palais train station is a charming, historic building located in the heart of the city. VIA Rail offers comfortable train service from Montreal, Ottawa, and other major cities in Canada.

- Navigating Gare du Palais: The train station is conveniently located near many hotels and attractions in the Old Town. You'll find taxis and public buses right outside the station, making it easy to reach your final destination.

By Car:

- Driving to Québec City: If you're traveling from within Canada or the northeastern United States, driving is a scenic option. Major highways connect Québec City to Montreal, Toronto, and other cities.

- Parking: Be aware that parking in the Old Town can be limited and expensive. Consider parking in a nearby lot or using public transportation to explore the historic center.

By Bus:

- Orléans Express: This bus company offers service to Québec City from various cities in Québec and Ontario. The bus terminal is located in Sainte-Foy, about a 20-minute drive from downtown.

- Navigating the Bus Terminal: From the Sainte-Foy bus terminal, you can take a taxi or public bus to reach your accommodation in Québec City.

Choosing Your Transportation:

The best mode of transportation depends on your budget, travel preferences, and starting point. If you're coming from overseas, flying into YQB is the most convenient option. For those traveling within Canada, the train offers a scenic and comfortable journey. If you're on a tight budget or enjoy road trips, consider taking the bus or driving.

No matter how you arrive, Québec City welcomes you with open arms!

City Transportation

Réseau de transport de la Capitale (RTC) Buses:

The RTC bus system is your main way to get around Québec City. It's reliable, affordable, and covers most areas of the city, including the Old Town, major attractions, and surrounding neighborhoods.

How to Buy Tickets and Passes:

- **Single Tickets:** These can be purchased directly from the bus driver with exact change (cash only). Be sure to ask for a transfer if you plan to switch buses within 90 minutes.

- **Day Passes:** A more economical option if you'll be taking multiple trips in a day. They can be purchased at the Grand Marché (market), tourist information centers, and some convenience stores.

- **Multi-Day Passes:** Available for unlimited travel over several days, a great choice for longer stays.

- **RTC Nomade App:** This app lets you buy and validate tickets directly on your smartphone, making it super convenient!

Fares:

A single bus ticket costs $3.50 CAD (approximately $2.60 USD) and a day pass is $8.50 CAD (approximately $6.30 USD). Prices may vary slightly, so check the RTC website or app for the most up-to-date information.

Other Transportation Options:

- **Taxis:** Readily available throughout the city, taxis can be hailed on the street or found at designated taxi stands.

- **Ride-Sharing:** Services like Uber and Lyft operate in Québec City, offering another convenient option for getting around.

- **Bike Rentals:** Several companies offer bike rentals, allowing you to explore the city at your own pace and enjoy the scenic bike paths.

- **Walking:** Québec City is incredibly pedestrian-friendly, especially in the Old Town. You can easily walk between many attractions, enjoying the charming streets and discovering hidden corners along the way.

Tips for Walking:

- **Stroll through the Old Town:** Take in the historic architecture, quaint shops, and lively squares.

- **Explore the Plains of Abraham:** Enjoy scenic walks with views of the St. Lawrence River.

- **Walk along the Ramparts:** These fortified walls offer a unique perspective of the city and its surroundings.

- **Descend to Lower Town via the Breakneck Stairs:** This steep but scenic staircase connects Upper Town and Lower Town.

By taking advantage of these transportation options, you'll be able to navigate Québec City with ease and make the most of your time exploring this charming destination.

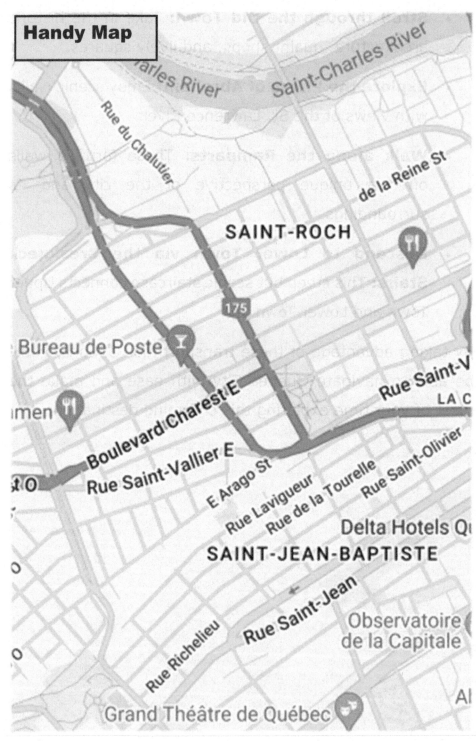

Handy Map

4. QUÉBEC CITY WITH KIDS

Family-Friendly Attractions: Family Fun in a Charming Setting

Québec City offers a delightful blend of history, culture, and outdoor adventures that will captivate both kids and adults. Here are some family-friendly attractions that will make your trip unforgettable:

Aquarium du Québec: Kids of all ages will be amazed by the Aquarium's diverse marine life, including seals, walruses, polar bears, and over 10,000 fish and invertebrates. There are also interactive exhibits, touch tanks, and outdoor play areas to keep the little ones entertained.

Village Vacances Valcartier: This massive amusement park is a thrill-seeker's paradise, with over 35 water slides, a wave pool, and a lazy river in the summer, and snow slides, skating, and tubing in the winter. It's a guaranteed fun-filled day for the whole family.

Plains of Abraham: This historic park offers plenty of space for kids to run and play, with expansive lawns, walking trails, and playgrounds. You can rent bikes, have a picnic, or simply enjoy the fresh air and stunning views of the St. Lawrence River.

Musée de la Civilisation: This interactive museum is a great place to learn about Québec's history and culture through engaging exhibits and hands-on activities. Kids will love exploring the Children's Museum, which features interactive displays and educational games.

Other Family-Friendly Options:

- **Parc de la Chute-Montmorency:** This park is home to the majestic Montmorency Falls, taller than Niagara Falls. Kids will be awestruck by the power and beauty of the falls, and there are plenty of trails for exploring.

- **Méga Parc:** This indoor amusement park features rides, games, and activities for all ages, making it a great option for a rainy day or when you need a break from the outdoors.

- **Erico Chocolate Factory and Chocolate Museum:** Take a sweet tour of this chocolate factory and learn how chocolate is made, from bean to bar. Kids (and adults!) will love the chance to sample delicious chocolates.

With its diverse range of attractions, Québec City offers endless fun and adventure for families. No matter what your interests, you're sure to find something that will delight everyone in your crew.

Kid-Approved Activities

Beyond the major attractions, there are plenty of other activities that will delight your little explorers:

Parc de la Chute-Montmorency (Montmorency Falls Park): Witness the awe-inspiring Montmorency Falls, even taller than Niagara Falls! Kids will be mesmerized by the roaring water and mist. Hike the trails, cross the suspension bridge for a thrilling view, or take a boat tour to get up close to the cascading water.

Boat Tour of the St. Lawrence River: Begin a family-friendly boat tour to see Québec City from a different perspective. Kids will love spotting landmarks like the Château Frontenac and the Citadelle, as well as watching for wildlife like seabirds and maybe even whales (depending on the season).

Playgrounds and Parks: Let the little ones loose in one of Québec City's many playgrounds and parks. Parc Jeanne-Mance, located in the heart of the city, offers a large playground, green spaces, and a wading pool in the summer.

Parc Victoria, near the Plains of Abraham, features a playground, a splash pad, and a skating rink in the winter.

Other Fun Activities:

- **Toboggan Slide Au 1884:** Experience the thrill of sliding down a giant ice slide on a wooden toboggan. It's a classic Québec City winter activity that kids (and adults!) will adore.

- **Méga Parc:** This indoor amusement park at the Galeries de la Capitale mall is a great option for a rainy day or when you need a break from the outdoors. It features rides, games, and a skating rink.

- **Plains of Abraham:** This historic park offers plenty of space for kids to run and play, with wide-open fields, walking paths, and a playground. Alternatively, discover the park by renting bicycles and pedaling around.

- **Visit a Sugar Shack:** During the spring maple syrup season, take the kids to a traditional sugar shack (cabane à sucre) for a sweet and sticky experience. They'll love tasting maple taffy on snow and learning about how maple syrup is made.

Québec City offers a diverse range of activities that cater to all ages and interests. With a little planning, you can create a fun-filled itinerary that will keep your kids entertained and engaged throughout your trip!

Tips for Traveling with Children

Traveling with kids can be its own exciting journey! But with a little planning and these handy tips, you can ensure a smooth and enjoyable experience for the whole family:

Packing for Kids:

- **Pack Light, But Be Prepared:** Bring essential clothing layers for unpredictable weather, comfortable shoes for exploring, and plenty of extra clothes for spills and messes.

- **Entertainment Essentials:** Pack a bag of games, books, coloring supplies, and small toys to keep kids occupied during travel time and downtime.

- **Snacks and Drinks:** Stock up on healthy snacks and drinks to avoid meltdowns and keep energy levels high. Remember to bring a reusable water bottle to keep yourself hydrated while out and about.

- **Comfort Items:** Bring along a favorite blanket, stuffed animal, or other comforting item to help your child feel secure in a new environment.

Kid-Friendly Restaurants:

- **Look for Casual Eateries:** Québec City has many casual restaurants and cafes with kid-friendly menus and relaxed atmospheres.

- **Check for Play Areas:** Some establishments offer play areas or children's menus with activities to keep kids entertained while you enjoy your meal.

- **Ask for Recommendations:** Don't hesitate to ask locals or hotel staff for recommendations on kid-friendly dining options.

Transportation with Strollers and Young Children:

- **Stroller Accessibility:** Québec City is generally stroller-friendly, with most sidewalks and attractions accessible. However, be prepared for some cobblestone streets and hills, especially in the Old Town.

- **Public Transportation:** The RTC bus system allows strollers on board, and some buses are equipped with ramps or low floors. However, it might be easier to navigate the city with a compact or lightweight stroller.

- **Taxis and Ride-Sharing:** If you have a lot of luggage or prefer a more convenient option, taxis and ride-sharing services are readily available.

Keeping Kids Entertained:

- **Embrace the Outdoors:** Québec City offers plenty of parks and playgrounds where kids can run, play, and explore.

- **Plan Interactive Activities:** Choose museums and attractions with hands-on exhibits or engaging programs for children.

- **Take Breaks:** Schedule regular breaks during sightseeing to let kids rest and recharge.

- **Let Them Choose:** Give children some choices in the activities and destinations, so they feel involved and excited about the trip.

By following these tips, you'll be well-equipped to navigate Québec City with kids in tow, creating lasting memories for the whole family.

5. MUST-SEE SIGHTS

Iconic Landmarks: Québec City's Crown Jewels

Château Frontenac

Dominating the Québec City skyline, the majestic Château Frontenac is an architectural masterpiece that exudes old-world elegance. This grand hotel, a National Historic Site of Canada, boasts fairytale-like turrets, copper roofs, and ornate interiors. It's no wonder it's the most photographed hotel in the world!

Originally built as a luxury hotel by the Canadian Pacific Railway in the late 19th century, the Château Frontenac has hosted royalty, dignitaries, and countless visitors from around the globe.

Best Spots for Photos & Views:

- The Dufferin Terrace: This expansive boardwalk offers breathtaking views of the St. Lawrence River and the Lower Town. The Château Frontenac serves as a stunning backdrop.

- The Château Frontenac Courtyard: Step into this charming courtyard for a closer look at the hotel's architecture and a different perspective of its grandeur.

- Inside the Château Frontenac: Explore the opulent lobby, grand staircase, and other public areas for a taste of luxury.

Guided Tours:

Take a guided tour to learn about the hotel's fascinating history, architectural details, and famous guests. You'll hear intriguing stories about Winston Churchill, Franklin D. Roosevelt, and other prominent figures who have stayed at the Château Frontenac.

Citadelle of Québec

Perched atop Cap Diamant, the star-shaped Citadelle is a formidable fortress that has protected Québec City for centuries. This UNESCO World Heritage Site is the oldest military building in Canada still in use.

Military Significance:

The Citadelle has played a crucial role in defending Québec City from attacks throughout history. Today, it's still an active military base and the official residence of the Governor General of Canada in Québec City.

Changing of the Guard Ceremony:

Don't miss the daily Changing of the Guard ceremony during the summer months, a colorful spectacle featuring marching soldiers, music, and precision drills. It's a fun and engaging experience for all ages.

Guided Tours:

Take a guided tour to explore the Citadelle's interior, learn about its military history, and discover hidden corners like the powder magazine and the officers' quarters.

Place Royale

Step into the heart of Old Québec at Place Royale, a charming square surrounded by historic buildings and steeped in history. This is where Québec City was founded in 1608 by Samuel de Champlain, and it remains a vibrant hub of activity today.

Birthplace of Québec City:

Place Royale was the center of New France's fur trade and the site of the first permanent French settlement in North America.

Notre-Dame-des-Victoires Church:

At the center of Place Royale, you'll find the beautiful Notre-Dame-des-Victoires Church, the oldest stone church in North America. Step inside to admire its intricate woodwork and stained glass windows.

These three iconic landmarks offer a glimpse into Québec City's rich history and cultural heritage. Each one is a must-see for any visitor to this enchanting city.

Charming Neighborhoods: Québec City's Hidden Treasure

Vieux-Québec (Old Town)

Prepare to be enchanted as you wander through the labyrinthine streets of Vieux-Québec, the historic heart of the city. Here, time seems to slow down as you admire the charming stone buildings, quaint shops, and lively squares.

Don't miss:

- **Rue du Petit-Champlain:** This pedestrian-only street is a shopper's paradise, lined with boutiques selling local crafts, gourmet food, and unique souvenirs.

- **Place d'Armes:** This lively square is a hub of activity, with street performers, outdoor cafes, and stunning views of the Château Frontenac.

- **Breakneck Stairs (Escalier Casse-Cou):** Descend these steep stairs for a fun adventure and a shortcut to Lower Town.

- **Artist's Alley (Rue du Trésor):** This narrow lane is a haven for local artists, where you can browse unique paintings, sculptures, and jewelry.

Saint-Jean-Baptiste

Just outside the city walls, the Saint-Jean-Baptiste neighborhood exudes a trendy, bohemian vibe. Its main street, Rue Saint-Jean, is a haven for foodies, with a wide array of cafes, restaurants, and gourmet shops.

Don't miss:

- **L'Affaire est Ketchup:** This popular restaurant serves up creative and delicious Québec cuisine in a cozy, bistro setting.

- **Le Hobbit Bistro:** A must-visit for Lord of the Rings fans, this quirky restaurant offers a hobbit-themed menu and ambiance.

- **J.A. Moisan Épicier:** This historic grocery store is a Québec City institution, offering a wide selection of local products and imported delicacies.

- **Plains of Abraham:** Take a stroll or have a picnic in this expansive park, which offers stunning views of the city and the St. Lawrence River.

Saint-Roch

Once a working-class neighborhood, Saint-Roch has transformed into a vibrant hub for artists and creatives. The area is bursting with colorful street art, trendy boutiques, and eclectic restaurants.

Don't miss:

- **Rue Saint-Joseph Est:** This main street is the heart of Saint-Roch, lined with shops selling vintage clothing, local designs, and artisanal goods.

- **La Barberie:** This popular microbrewery is a great place to sample local craft beers and enjoy a lively atmosphere.

- **Le Clocher Penché:** This former church is now a multi-functional arts center hosting concerts, theater performances, and exhibitions.

These three neighborhoods offer a glimpse into the diverse and dynamic spirit of Québec City. Each one has its unique charm and attractions, waiting to be discovered.

Cultural Hotspots

Musée de la Civilisation

Prepare to be inspired by the Musée de la Civilisation, a fascinating museum that delves into the heart of Québec's history, culture, and society. Through engaging exhibits, interactive displays, and thought-provoking artifacts, you'll gain a deeper understanding of this unique region and its people.

Don't miss:

- **Permanent Exhibits:** Explore the diverse exhibits that showcase Québec's rich history, from its Indigenous roots to its French colonial past and modern identity. Learn about the province's traditions, arts, and social movements through a variety of multimedia displays, artifacts, and interactive installations.

- **Temporary Exhibits:** Check the museum's website for current temporary exhibits, which often focus on contemporary issues, global cultures, or specific aspects of Québec's heritage.

- **Family-Friendly Activities:** The museum offers a range of activities and programs designed for families, including workshops, guided tours, and interactive exhibits. The Children's Museum is a must-visit for little ones, with its hands-on displays and playful learning experiences.

Musée National des Beaux-Arts du Québec

Engage yourself in the world of art at the Musée National des Beaux-Arts du Québec, a renowned institution that houses a vast collection of Québec and Canadian art. From historical paintings and sculptures to contemporary works and installations, the museum offers a comprehensive overview of the region's artistic achievements.

Don't miss:

- **Permanent Collection:** Explore the museum's impressive collection, which spans over 42,000 works of art. You'll find masterpieces by renowned Québec artists like Jean-Paul Riopelle, Alfred Pellan, and Jean Paul Lemieux, as well as works by other Canadian and international artists.

- **Temporary Exhibitions:** The museum regularly hosts temporary exhibitions that showcase a variety of artistic styles and movements. Check the website for the latest schedule and themes.

- **Sculpture Garden:** Stroll through the picturesque sculpture garden, where you can admire a collection of modern and contemporary sculptures set against the backdrop of the St. Lawrence River.

These two cultural hotspots offer a glimpse into Québec City's artistic soul, showcasing its rich history, diverse cultural heritage, and vibrant contemporary art scene.

Natural Escapes

Plains of Abraham

The Plains of Abraham are a historic park in Quebec City, Canada. The Plains were the site of two major battles during the Seven Years' War, the Battle of the Plains of Abraham in 1759 and the Battle of Sainte-Foy in 1760. Today, the Plains are a popular spot for picnics, walking, cycling, and cross-country skiing.

How to get there:

The Plains of Abraham are located in the center of Quebec City. You can walk or bike to the Plains from most parts of the city. You have the option of taking the bus or cable car.

Best viewing points:

There are many great places to view the Plains of Abraham. Some of the best include:

- The Dufferin Terrace: This terrace offers stunning views of the Plains and the St. Lawrence River.

- The Terrasse de la Citadelle: This terrace offers views of the Plains and the city of Quebec.

- The Battlefields Park: This park is home to a number of monuments and memorials, including the Martello Towers and the Jeanne d'Arc statue.

Optional activities:

There are a number of optional activities that you can enjoy at the Plains of Abraham, including:

- Visiting the Musée des plaines d'Abraham: This museum tells the story of the Plains of Abraham and the battles that were fought there.

- Taking a walk or bike ride on the Plains: The Plains are a great place to go for a walk or bike ride. There are a number of trails that you can follow, or you can just explore the park at your own pace.

- Having a picnic: The Plains are a great place to have a picnic. There are a number of picnic tables located throughout the park, or you can find a spot on the grass and enjoy the view.

Montmorency Falls

Montmorency Falls is a waterfall located just outside of Quebec City, Canada. The falls are 83 meters (272 feet) tall and are twice as high as Niagara Falls. Montmorency Falls is a popular tourist destination and is home to a number of attractions, including:

- The Montmorency Falls Park: This park offers a variety of activities, including hiking, ziplining, and rock climbing.

- The Montmorency Falls Cable Car: This cable car takes you to the top of the falls for stunning views.

- The Montmorency Falls Bridge: This bridge offers views of the falls from below.

How to get there:

Montmorency Falls is located just outside of Quebec City. You can take the bus or drive to the falls. The bus journey is approximately 30 minutes long.

Best viewing points:

There are many great places to view Montmorency Falls. Some of the best include:

- The viewing platform at the top of the falls: This platform offers stunning views of the falls and the surrounding area.

- The bridge over the falls: This bridge offers views of the falls from below.

- The hiking trails: There are a number of hiking trails that lead to different viewpoints of the falls.

Optional activities:

There are a number of optional activities that you can enjoy at Montmorency Falls, including:

- Taking a walk or hike on the trails: There are a number of trails that lead to different viewpoints of the falls.

- Going ziplining: There is a zipline that takes you over the falls.

- Going rock climbing: There are a number of rock climbing routes near the falls.

- Having a picnic: There are a number of picnic tables located near the falls.

6. OFF-THE-BEATEN-PATH

Hidden Gems & Local Secrets

Tired of the crowds? Venture beyond the well-trodden tourist path and uncover Québec City's hidden gems, where local secrets and unique experiences await.

Morrin Centre:

Step back in time at the Morrin Centre, a fascinating building with a storied past. Originally built as a prison in the 1800s, it later became a college and now houses a cultural center and English-language library. Explore the eerie jail cells, wander through the Victorian library, and discover the center's rich history through exhibits and guided tours. It's a truly unique glimpse into Québec City's past.

Rue Couillard:

Tucked away in the Old City, Rue Couillard is a charming street lined with art galleries, antique shops, and historic homes. This hidden gem is perfect for leisurely strolls and discovering unique treasures. Browse the eclectic mix of art, from paintings and sculptures to jewelry and ceramics, or search for antique furniture, books, and other curiosities. You might even stumble upon a cozy café or hidden courtyard where you can relax and soak up the atmosphere.

Parc du Bois-de-Coulonge:

Escape the hustle and bustle of the city and find tranquility at Parc du Bois-de-Coulonge. This sprawling park is a haven for nature lovers, with beautifully manicured gardens, serene walking trails, and a tranquil lake. It's a perfect spot for a picnic, a leisurely stroll, or simply enjoying the peace and quiet of nature.

Bonus Tip: If you're visiting during the summer months, be sure to check out the park's outdoor theater, which hosts concerts and other events throughout the season.

These are just a few of the hidden gems waiting to be discovered in Québec City. Venture off the beaten path, and you'll be rewarded with unforgettable experiences and a deeper understanding of this enchanting city.

Unique Experiences

Savor a Sugar Shack Feast:

Experience a true taste of Québec tradition at a *cabane à sucre* (sugar shack). These rustic restaurants, often located in the countryside surrounding Québec City, serve up hearty meals featuring maple syrup in every imaginable form. From maple-glazed ham and baked beans to maple taffy pulled on snow, it's a sweet and savory feast that's sure to delight your taste buds. Many sugar shacks also offer live music, folk dancing, and horse-drawn sleigh rides for a truly captivating experience.

Cheer on the Québec Remparts at a Hockey Game:

Hockey is more than just a sport in Québec City; it's a way of life. Join the passionate fans at the Videotron Centre to cheer on the Québec Remparts, the city's major junior hockey team. The atmosphere is electric, with roaring crowds, thundering chants, and a palpable energy that will make you feel like a true local. Even if you're not a hockey fan, it's an unforgettable experience that captures the spirit of Québec City.

More Unique Experiences to Consider:

- **Explore the Ice Hotel:** During the winter months, the Hôtel de Glace, a hotel made entirely of ice and snow, is a must-see. Take a tour, sip a cocktail in an ice glass, or even spend the night in a sub-zero room.

- **Wander Through the German Christmas Market:** Lose yourself in the festive spirit at the German Christmas Market, held annually in Old Québec during the holiday season. Sample traditional German treats, browse unique crafts, and enjoy the enchanting atmosphere.

- **Discover Local Art:** Québec City has a thriving arts scene, with numerous galleries and studios showcasing the work of local artists. Take a stroll through the art-filled streets of Saint-Roch or visit the annual Plein Art Québec festival to discover hidden talents.

By embracing these unique experiences, you'll truly engage with the heart and soul of Québec City, creating memories that will last a lifetime.

7. LOCAL FLAVORS

Must-Try Dishes: A Taste of Québec

Poutine: The Québec Icon

No trip to Québec City is complete without savoring its most iconic dish: poutine. This hearty and comforting creation features crispy French fries topped with fresh cheese curds and smothered in rich, flavorful gravy. The result is a delicious symphony of textures and tastes that will leave you craving more.

While the exact origin of poutine is debated, it's undeniable that this dish has become a beloved symbol of Québec's culinary identity. You'll find poutine served in

countless variations across the city, from classic to gourmet.

Where to Find the Best Poutine:

- **Chez Ashton:** This local institution has been serving up classic poutine since the 1960s. Their generous portions and perfectly balanced combination of fries, curds, and gravy have earned them a loyal following.

Address: 54 Côte du Palais, Québec, QC G1R 4H8, Canada.
Phone number is +1 418-692-3055.

- **La Banquise:** A popular late-night spot, La Banquise offers over 30 different poutine creations, from traditional to wildly inventive. Try the "T-Rex" with ground beef, pepperoni, bacon, and hot dog for a truly indulgent experience.

Address: 994 Rue Rachel E, Montréal, QC H2J 2J3,
Canada. Phone number is +1 514-525-2415.

- **Le Chic Shack:** For a gourmet twist on poutine, head to Le Chic Shack, where you'll find creative concoctions like duck confit poutine and lobster poutine.

Address: 15 Rue du Fort, Québec, QC G1R 3Z8, Canada.
Phone number: +1 418-692-1485.

Other Must-Try Dishes:

While poutine reigns supreme, Québec City boasts a rich culinary scene with many other delicious dishes to discover:

- **Tourtière:** A savory meat pie traditionally made with pork, veal, or beef, flavored with spices like cloves, nutmeg, and cinnamon.

- **Creton:** A spreadable pork pâté seasoned with onions and spices, typically served on toast for breakfast or brunch.

- **Fèves au Lard:** A hearty bean dish cooked with salt pork or bacon, often served as a side dish or in a soup.

- **Tarte au Sucre (Sugar Pie):** A sweet and simple dessert made with maple syrup, brown sugar, and cream.

- **Cipaille:** A layered meat pie made with wild game or beef, potatoes, and onions. It's a hearty and flavorful dish that reflects Québec's culinary heritage.

- **Grands-Pères au Sirop d'Érable (Maple Syrup Dumplings):** These fluffy dumplings are simmered in a sweet maple syrup sauce and served warm.

Traditional Restaurants

For an authentic taste of Québec's culinary heritage, venture beyond the poutine joints and explore these traditional restaurants:

- **Aux Anciens Canadiens:** Housed in a charming 17th-century building, this iconic restaurant serves up classic Québécois dishes like tourtière, cipaille, and maple syrup pie in a cozy, historic setting.

> *Address: 34 Rue Saint-Louis, Québec, QC G1R 4P3, Canada*
> *Phone: +1 418-692-1627*

- **La Buche:** With two locations in Old Québec, this rustic eatery embraces Québec's sugar shack traditions, offering hearty dishes like maple-baked beans, pea soup, and maple syrup pudding in a warm, wood-paneled ambiance

> *Address 1: 49 Rue Saint-Louis, Québec, QC G1R 3Z2, Canada*
> *Phone 1: +1 418-694-1884*
> *Address 2: 10 Rue Saint-Nicolas, Québec, QC G1K 4E1, Canada*
> *Phone 2: +1 418-525-9229*

- **Le Buffet de l'Antiquaire:** Step back in time at this charming restaurant in the Old Port, where you can feast on traditional Québec fare like meatball stew, pea soup, and sugar pie, all served buffet-style.

Address: 95 Rue Saint-Paul, Québec, QC G1K 3V8, Canada
Phone: +1 418-692-2661

- **Cochon Dingue:** With several locations across the city, this popular restaurant chain offers a modern twist on classic Québécois dishes, using fresh, local ingredients and creative culinary techniques.

Address: 46 Boulevard Champlain, Québec, QC G1K 4E8, Canada
Phone Number: +1 418-692-2013

- **Le Continental:** This family-owned establishment has been serving up hearty Québécois cuisine for over 50 years. Their menu features classics like poutine, tourtière, and maple-glazed ham, as well as daily specials and a warm, welcoming atmosphere.

Address: 26 Rue Saint-Louis, Québec, QC G1R 3Y8, Canada
Phone: +1 418-694-9995

By sampling these local specialties, you'll get a true taste of Québec City's unique culinary heritage. However, these are just a few of the many traditional restaurants where you can experience the rich flavors and warm hospitality of Québec City's culinary scene. Bon appétit!

Markets & Shops: Where to Shop & What to Shop

Québec City offers a delightful shopping experience, from bustling markets to charming boutiques and specialty shops. Here are some must-visit spots for finding unique treasures and souvenirs:

Grand Marché de Québec: This bustling market is a feast for the senses, filled with colorful displays of fresh local produce, artisanal cheeses, baked goods, maple syrup products, and handcrafted souvenirs. Wander through the stalls, sample local delicacies, and chat with friendly vendors. You're sure to find something to tempt your taste buds or take home as a reminder of your Québec City adventure.

Address: section M, 250 Bd Wilfrid-Hamel, Québec, QC G1L 5A7, Canada.
Open 9AM to 5PM Monday to Sunday.

Quartier Petit Champlain: This picturesque neighborhood, nestled at the foot of the cliff below Château Frontenac, is a shopper's paradise. Stroll along its narrow, cobblestone streets and discover charming boutiques selling Québec-made clothing, jewelry, art, and other unique gifts. Don't miss the chance to pop into a cozy café or chocolate shop for a sweet treat!

Address: 61 Rue du Petit Champlain, Québec, QC G1K 4H5, Canada
Open 10AM to 5PM Monday to Sunday

Shops Specializing in Local Crafts, Art, or Maple Products:

- **La Petite Cabane à Sucre de Québec:** This shop in the Old Town specializes in maple products, from syrup and candy to cookies and spreads. It's the perfect place to pick up a sweet souvenir or gift.

Address: 94 Rue du Petit Champlain, Québec, QC G1K 4H4, Canada.
Open 9:30AM to 5:30PM Monday to Sunday, 9:30AM to 9PM Thursday to Friday.

- **La Maison Simons:** This department store, a Québec City institution, offers a wide range of clothing, home goods, and accessories, including a curated selection of local designers.

> *Address: 977 Rue Sainte-Catherine, Montréal, QC H3B 4W3, Canada.*
> *Open 10AM to 6:30PM Monday to Saturday, 10AM to 9PM Thursday and Friday, 10AM to 6PM Sunday.*

- **Galerie d'Art Inuit Brousseau et Brousseau:** Discover the beauty of Inuit art at this gallery, which showcases sculptures, prints, and other works by Indigenous artists from across Canada.

> *Address: 35 Rue Saint-Louis, Québec, QC G1R 3Z2, Canada. Open 9:30AM to 5:30PM Monday to Sunday.*

- **Marché de Noël Allemand de Québec (German Christmas Market):** If you're visiting during the holiday season, don't miss this festive market, where you can find unique gifts, decorations, and traditional German treats.

> *Address: 7 Rue Pierre-Olivier-Chauveau, Québec, QC G1R 5M1, Canada.*

Other Shopping Tips:

- **Look for the "Produit du Québec" Label:** This label indicates that a product is made in Québec, ensuring you're supporting local artisans and businesses.

- **Haggle at Flea Markets:** If you're a bargain hunter, check out the flea markets held in various locations throughout the city. You might just score a unique find at a great price.

- **Take Advantage of Tax Refunds:** As a visitor to Canada, you may be eligible for a tax refund on your purchases. Ask for a tax-free form at the store and follow the instructions for claiming your refund at the airport or border crossing.

With its diverse array of shopping options, Québec City is sure to satisfy your retail therapy cravings and leave you with lasting memories (and souvenirs!) of your trip.

Cafés & Restaurants

Québec City's food scene is as diverse as its history and culture, offering something to tempt every palate and budget. Below is a glimpse of what you can anticipate:

Casual Cafés:

- **La Maison Smith:** This local chain is a favorite for its expertly brewed coffee, fresh pastries, and cozy atmosphere. Multiple locations throughout the city make it a convenient stop for a caffeine fix and a sweet treat.

Locations: 750 Rue Saint-Jean, Québec City, QC G1R 1P8, Canada
23 Rue Notre Dame, Québec, QC G1K 4E9, Canada

- **Paillard:** Indulge in delicious croissants, sandwiches, and other baked goods at this popular bakery and café.

Address: 1097 Rue Saint-Jean, Québec City, QC G1R 1S3, Canada

- **Nektar Caféologue:** Coffee aficionados will appreciate this café's dedication to quality beans and expertly crafted brews.

Locations: 235 Rue Saint-Joseph Est (Saint-Roch) and 567 Rue Saint-Jean (Saint-Jean-Baptiste)

Family-Friendly Restaurants:

- **Le Cochon Dingue:** With a menu featuring classic Québec dishes and a lively atmosphere, this restaurant chain is a hit with families.

- **Casse-Croûte Pierrot:** This casual eatery offers burgers, hot dogs, poutine, and other kid-friendly favorites at affordable prices.

- **Le Chic Shack:** This popular spot is known for its gourmet burgers, milkshakes, and creative poutine variations.

Fine Dining Establishments:

- **Laurie Raphaël:** For an upscale culinary experience, this elegant restaurant offers innovative tasting menus showcasing local ingredients and refined techniques.

- **iXu:** This Asian-fusion restaurant blends traditional Japanese cuisine with modern flavors and artistic presentations.

- **Légende par la Tanière:** This intimate restaurant celebrates Indigenous cuisine, offering a unique and flavorful dining experience.

Restaurants with Unique Atmospheres or Views:

- **Le Lapin Sauté:** Nestled in the heart of Petit Champlain, this charming restaurant specializes in rabbit dishes served in a cozy, rustic setting.

- **Le Café du Monde:** Enjoy breathtaking views of the St. Lawrence River and Île d'Orléans while savoring classic French cuisine at this elegant bistro.

- **L'Échaudé:** Step back in time at this restaurant housed in a historic building, where you can dine on traditional Québécois dishes by candlelight.

8. QUÉBEC CITY AFTER DARK

Bars & Pubs for Every Taste

When the sun sets, Québec City's nightlife scene comes alive, offering a diverse array of bars and pubs to suit every mood and preference.

Lively Pubs in the Old City (Vieux-Québec):

- **Pub Saint-Patrick:** This Irish pub is a popular gathering spot for locals and tourists alike. With its warm, welcoming atmosphere, live music, and wide selection of beers, it's the perfect place to unwind and soak up the local pub culture.

- **Pub L'Oncle Antoine:** Located in a 300-year-old building, this historic pub exudes charm and character. Sip on local craft beers, enjoy traditional Québécois snacks, and mingle with friendly patrons in a cozy, intimate setting.

Trendy Bars in Saint-Roch:

- **L'Anti Bar & Spectacles:** This hip bar is a favorite among the local arts and music scene. Enjoy live music, DJs, and other events while sipping on creative cocktails and craft beers.

- **Le Sacrilège:** This stylish bar is known for its extensive selection of microbrews, artisanal cocktails, and delicious tapas. The industrial-chic décor and intimate atmosphere make it a perfect spot for a romantic evening or a night out with friends.

- **La Korrigane:** This popular microbrasserie serves up a variety of its own craft beers, along with a menu of hearty pub fare. The lively atmosphere and communal tables make it a great place to meet fellow beer enthusiasts.

Bars with Live Music & Entertainment:

- **Le Cercle:** This iconic music venue hosts a diverse range of live music acts, from local bands to international artists. Check their calendar for upcoming shows and get ready for a night of unforgettable entertainment.

- **L'Impérial Bell:** Another beloved music venue, L'Impérial Bell showcases a variety of genres, including rock, pop, indie, and electronic music. With its state-of-the-art sound system and intimate setting, it's a top spot for music lovers.

Bonus Tip: Many bars and pubs in Québec City offer happy hour specials, so be sure to ask about them when you arrive. It's a great way to sample local drinks and save a few bucks!

No matter what your style, you're sure to find the perfect spot to enjoy Québec City's vibrant nightlife. So, raise a glass to good times and unforgettable memories!

Live Music & Entertainment:

The fun doesn't stop when the sun goes down in Québec City. The city's music scene comes alive at night, with a wide range of venues catering to diverse tastes.

Major Concert Halls:

- **Grand Théâtre de Québec:** This impressive performing arts complex hosts a variety of shows, including operas, ballets, symphony orchestras, and plays. Its two halls offer world-class acoustics and elegant settings, ensuring a memorable experience.

- **Palais Montcalm:** Located in the heart of Old Québec, this historic theater presents a diverse program of classical music, jazz, dance, and other performances. Its intimate atmosphere and excellent acoustics create a special connection between performers and audience.

Smaller Venues with Local Flavor:

- **Le Scanner:** This trendy bistro-bar in Saint-Roch is a hub for emerging local bands and artists. Enjoy live music, DJs, and other events while sipping on craft beers and cocktails.

- **L'Anti Bar & Spectacles:** This alternative bar in Saint-Roch hosts a wide range of musical genres, from rock and punk to folk and electronic. It's a great place to discover new talent and experience Québec City's underground music scene.

- **Le D'Auteuil:** Nestled in the heart of the Old City, this cozy bar features live jazz performances most nights of the week. It's the perfect spot to unwind with a drink and enjoy smooth tunes in a relaxed setting.

- **Le Drague Cabaret Club:** If you're looking for a unique and entertaining experience, check out this lively cabaret club, which features drag shows, burlesque performances, and other themed nights.

Additional Live Music Options:

- **Many pubs and bars** in the Old Town and Saint-Jean-Baptiste neighborhoods offer live music on certain nights. Keep an eye out for posters and flyers advertising local bands and performers.

- **During the summer months,** Québec City hosts numerous outdoor concerts and festivals, including the Festival d'été de Québec, which features world-renowned musical acts on multiple stages.

Festivals & Events

Québec City's calendar is packed with exciting festivals and events that showcase the city's vibrant culture and unique traditions. Here are some highlights:

Winter:

- **Québec Winter Carnival (Carnaval de Québec):** This world-famous festival transforms the city into a winter wonderland, with dazzling ice sculptures, snow slides, parades, and a host of outdoor activities. Don't miss the chance to meet Bonhomme Carnaval, the festival's iconic mascot!

- **Québec City International Pee-Wee Hockey Tournament:** Young hockey players from around the world compete in this prestigious tournament, which is a beloved tradition in Québec City.

Spring:

- **Maple Syrup Season:** In the spring, sugar shacks across the region open their doors to visitors, offering delicious maple-themed meals and activities.

- **Festival des traditions du monde de Sherbrooke:** This multicultural festival celebrates traditions from around the globe with music, dance, food, and crafts.

Summer:

- **Festival d'été de Québec (FEQ):** One of North America's largest music festivals, FEQ features world-renowned artists performing on multiple stages throughout the city.

- **New France Festival (Les Fêtes de la Nouvelle-France):** Step back in time to the 17th and 18th centuries during this historical festival, which celebrates Québec City's French colonial roots with re-enactments, period costumes, and traditional music and dance.

- **Les Grands Feux Loto-Québec:** This spectacular fireworks competition lights up the sky over the St. Lawrence River every Wednesday and Saturday night during the summer.

Fall:

- **Quebec City Celtic Festival:** This lively festival celebrates Celtic culture with music, dance, storytelling, and traditional food and drink.

- **Envol et Macadam:** This alternative music festival showcases emerging talent from Québec and beyond, featuring punk, rock, metal, and other genres.

Other Notable Events:

- **Wendake International Pow Wow:** This annual event celebrates Indigenous culture with traditional dance, music, food, and crafts.

- **ComediHa! Fest-Québec:** This comedy festival features stand-up comedians, improv troupes, and other comedic performances from around the world.

Whether you're a fan of music, history, culture, or simply enjoy a lively atmosphere, Québec City's festivals and events offer something for everyone. Check the city's event calendar to see what's happening during your visit.

9. DAY TRIPS & EXCURSIONS

Île d'Orléans

Île d'Orléans is a charming island located in the Saint Lawrence River, just across from Québec City. It's known for its rural charm, picturesque villages, and scenic landscapes.

Here's how to get to Île d'Orléans from Québec City:

By car:

It's a short and easy drive from Québec City to Île d'Orléans. Take Route 138 east until you reach the Île d'Orléans Bridge. The bridge is free to cross, and the drive takes about 30 minutes.

By bike:

If you're feeling adventurous, you can also bike to Île d'Orléans. The ride takes about 1 hour and 15 minutes, and there's a dedicated bike lane on the bridge.

Once you're on the island, you can explore the many charming villages, visit farms, taste local produce, and enjoy outdoor activities like cycling and kayaking.

Here's a suggested route for exploring the island:

- Start your day in Sainte-Pétronille, the oldest village on the island. Visit the beautiful Sainte-Pétronille Church, which was built in 1749.

- Next, head to Saint-François, where you can visit the Maison d'Expérimentation Agricole, a working farm that offers tours and tastings of local products.

- Continue to Saint-Pierre, the largest village on the island. Be sure to check out the Chocolaterie de l'Île d'Orléans, which makes delicious chocolates using locally-sourced ingredients.

- Finally, head to Sainte-Famille, where you can visit the Moulin de la Pointe, a restored windmill that is now a museum.

This is just a suggested route, of course, and there are many other things to see and do on Île d'Orléans. Be sure to take your time and explore the island at your own pace.

Montmorency Falls Park

Prepare to be awestruck by the sheer power and beauty of Montmorency Falls, a natural wonder located just a short

drive from Québec City. Plunging 83 meters (272 feet) into the St. Lawrence River, these cascading falls are a sight to behold, even surpassing the height of Niagara Falls!

Different Ways to Experience the Falls:

- **Viewing Platforms:** Multiple platforms offer different perspectives of the falls. The panoramic view from the top is breathtaking, while the lower platform lets you feel the mist on your face.

- **Cable Car (Manoir Montmorency):** Glide up to the top of the cliff in a cable car for stunning panoramic views of the falls, the river, and the surrounding landscape.

- **Suspended Bridge:** Take a thrilling walk across the suspended bridge that stretches above the crest of the falls. Feel the spray of the water and marvel at the sheer power of nature.

- **Boat Tour:** Embark on a boat tour for an up-close and personal encounter with the falls. Feel the mist on your face and hear the thunderous roar as you approach the base of this natural wonder.

Activities in the Park:

- **Hiking:** Explore the park's network of trails that wind through the forest and offer various viewpoints of the falls.

- **Picnicking:** Enjoy a scenic picnic on the grassy lawns overlooking the falls. There are several picnic tables and shelters available.

- **Ziplining:** For the adventurous, soar above the falls on a thrilling zipline experience.

Tips for Visiting:

- **Wear comfortable shoes:** There's a lot of walking involved, especially if you plan on hiking.

- **Bring a rain jacket or poncho:** The mist from the falls can get you wet, even on a sunny day.

- **Consider visiting during the evening:** The falls are illuminated at night, creating a magical ambiance.

Montmorency Falls Park is a must-visit destination for any nature lover. Its dramatic beauty, diverse activities, and proximity to Québec City make it an unforgettable experience.

Wendake Huron Village

Just a short drive from Québec City lies Wendake, the urban reserve of the Huron-Wendat Nation.

This vibrant community welcomes visitors to explore their rich culture, history, and traditions.

The Huron-Wendat Nation:

The Huron-Wendat people have inhabited the Québec region for centuries. Their ancestral lands once stretched across a vast territory, and their culture is deeply rooted in nature, spirituality, and community. Today, the Huron-Wendat Nation is a thriving community that preserves its traditions while embracing modernity.

Cultural Attractions in Wendake:

- **Huron Traditional Site (Onhoüa Chetek8e):** This reconstructed Huron village offers a fascinating glimpse into the daily life and customs of the Huron-Wendat people. Explore traditional longhouses, learn about their ancient way of life, and witness demonstrations of traditional crafts like canoe making and beadwork.

- **Notre-Dame-de-Lorette Church:** This beautiful church, built in 1730, is a testament to the Huron-

Wendat's Catholic faith. Admire its unique architecture, which blends European and Indigenous elements.

- **Kabir Kouba Falls:** These picturesque waterfalls are a sacred site for the Huron-Wendat people. Take a peaceful walk along the trails, enjoy the natural beauty, and learn about the cultural significance of the falls.

- **Hôtel-Musée Premières Nations:** This unique hotel and museum showcases contemporary Indigenous art and culture. Stay overnight in one of the stylish rooms decorated with Indigenous artwork, or simply visit the museum to explore the exhibits and learn about the rich history and traditions of the Huron-Wendat people.

Cultural Experiences:

- **Attend a Cultural Performance:** Throughout the year, Wendake hosts various cultural events, including traditional dance performances, storytelling sessions, and music concerts. Check the community's event calendar for upcoming performances.

- **Try Traditional Huron Cuisine:** Savor the flavors of Huron-Wendat cuisine at one of the local restaurants.

Sample dishes like bannock (a type of flatbread), wild game stews, and maple-infused desserts.

Visiting Wendake is a unique opportunity to learn about Indigenous culture and history in a respectful and engaging way. Engage yourself in the traditions, explore the natural beauty, and connect with the warm hospitality of the Huron-Wendat people.

10. ACCOMMODATIONS

Québec City offers a diverse range of accommodations to suit every budget and taste, from charming historic inns to modern boutique hotels, cozy bed and breakfasts, and budget-friendly hostels.

Budget-Friendly Options:

1. **Auberge Internationale de Québec:** Centrally located hostel with a lively atmosphere, perfect for solo travelers and budget-minded visitors.

   - **Price Range:** $25-50 USD per night

   - **Address:** 19 Rue Ste-Ursule, Québec, QC G1R 4E1, Canada

   - **Phone:** +1 418-694-0755

   - **Facilities:** Dorms and private rooms, communal kitchen, common areas, free Wi-Fi, laundry facilities, bike rentals.

- **About:** Known for its social atmosphere, organized activities, and central location near attractions and nightlife.

2. **HI Québec City:** Modern hostel with comfortable rooms and communal spaces, ideal for social travelers seeking a convenient and affordable stay.

- **Price Range:** $30-60 USD per night

- **Address:** 19 Rue Ste-Ursule, Québec, QC G1R 4E1, Canada

- **Phone:** +1 418-694-0755

- **Facilities:** Dorms and private rooms, communal kitchen, common areas, free Wi-Fi, laundry facilities, bike rentals, outdoor patio.

- **About:** Offers a mix of private and shared rooms, organized activities, and a friendly staff.

3. **Gîte Sun Of a Beach:** Relaxed and budget-friendly guesthouse with a laid-back vibe, ideal for travelers seeking a simple and affordable accommodation.

- **Price Range:** $40-70 USD per night

- **Address:** 67 Rue Dauphine, Québec, QC G1K 4E2, Canada

- **Phone:** +1 418-692-5881

- **Facilities:** Simple rooms, shared kitchen, common areas, free Wi-Fi, garden.

- **About:** A cozy option with a focus on community and budget-friendly rates.

4. **Auberge Maeva:** Small and cozy hostel with a warm, welcoming atmosphere and a rooftop terrace offering views of the city.

- **Price Range:** $25-50 USD per night

- **Address:** 135 Rue Saint-Vallier Ouest, Québec, QC G1K 1J8, Canada

- **Phone:** +1 418-525-9229

- **Facilities:** Dorms and private rooms, communal kitchen, common areas, free Wi-Fi, terrace.

> - **About:** A family-run hostel with a focus on creating a friendly and social environment.

5. **Hôtel Le Voyageur:** Basic hotel with clean rooms and a convenient location near the bus terminal, perfect for travelers on a budget.

- **Price Range:** $60-100 USD per night
- **Address:** 1155 Rue de la Chevrotière, Québec, QC G1K 3P4, Canada
- **Phone:** +1 418-525-6028
- **Facilities:** Simple rooms with private bathrooms, free Wi-Fi, continental breakfast.
- **About:** A no-frills option that prioritizes affordability and convenience.

Mid-Range Choices:

6. **Hôtel Le Priori:** Stylish hotel in the Old Town with cozy, individually decorated rooms, exposed brick walls, and modern amenities.

- **Price Range:** $120-200 USD per night

- **Address:** 15 Rue Sainte-Anne, Québec, QC G1R 3X2, Canada

- **Phone:** +1 418-692-0952

- **Facilities:** Comfortable rooms, free Wi-Fi, on-site restaurant, bar.

- **About:** Offers a charming and historic ambiance with contemporary comforts.

7. **Hôtel Manoir Victoria:** Elegant hotel in the city center with spacious rooms, a rooftop terrace with city views, indoor pool, fitness center, and on-site restaurant.

- **Price Range:** $150-250 USD per night

- **Address:** 44 Côte du Palais, Québec, QC G1R 4H8, Canada

- **Phone:** +1 418-692-1030

- **Facilities:** Variety of rooms and suites, free Wi-Fi, indoor pool, fitness center, restaurant, bar, spa services.

- **About:** A luxurious stay with excellent amenities and a central location.

8. **Hôtel Palace Royal:** Modern hotel located steps from the Château Frontenac, offering comfortable rooms with city views and a variety of amenities.

- **Price Range:** $130-220 USD per night

- **Address:** 775 Rue Honoré-Mercier, Québec, QC G1R 5A5, Canada

- **Phone:** +1 418-694-2000

- **Facilities:** Modern rooms, free Wi-Fi, indoor pool, fitness center, restaurant, bar.

- **About:** A contemporary option with a focus on convenience and comfort.

9. **Hôtel Clarendon:** Historic hotel with classic charm and modern amenities, located in the heart of the Old Town, offering a taste of Québec City's heritage.

- **Price Range:** $150-250 USD per night

- **Address:** 57 Rue Sainte-Anne, Québec, QC G1R 3X2, Canada

- **Phone:** +1 418-692-2480

- **Facilities:** Classic rooms, free Wi-Fi, on-site restaurant, bar.

- **About:** A charming and elegant hotel with a rich history and a central location.

10. **Hôtel Le Concorde Québec:** Large hotel with a wide range of rooms and suites, ideal for families and groups seeking a comfortable stay with various on-site amenities.

- **Price Range:** $100-200 USD per night

- **Address:** 1225 Cours du Général-de Montcalm, Québec, QC G1R 4W6, Canada

- **Phone:** +1 418-647-2222

- **Facilities:** Various room types, free Wi-Fi, indoor pool, fitness center, multiple restaurants and bars, business center.

- **About:** Offers a variety of amenities and services to cater to diverse needs.

11. **Auberge Saint-Antoine:** Luxury hotel built around an archaeological site, offering elegant rooms with exposed stone walls and original artifacts.

- **Price Range:** $300-500+ USD per night

- **Address:** 8 Rue Saint-Antoine, Québec, QC G1K 4C9, Canada

- **Phone:** +1 418-692-2211

- **Facilities:** Luxurious rooms and suites, on-site restaurant and bar, spa, fitness center, meeting rooms, historic artifacts on display.

- **About:** A unique blend of history and modern luxury, with exceptional service and a prime location in the Old Port.

12. Hôtel 71: Chic hotel in a former bank building, featuring contemporary design, a rooftop terrace with city views, and a renowned restaurant.

- **Price Range:** $250-450+ USD per night

- **Address:** 71 Rue Saint-Pierre, Québec, QC G1K 4A4, Canada

- **Phone:** +1 418-692-1171

- **Facilities:** Stylish rooms and suites, free Wi-Fi, rooftop terrace, fitness center, on-site restaurant, bar.

- **About:** A modern and sophisticated hotel with a prime location in the Old Port, perfect for design-conscious travelers.

13. Le Monastère des Augustines: Tranquil hotel and wellness center housed in a former monastery, offering simple yet elegant rooms and access to a museum, spa, and healthy cuisine.

- **Price Range:** $150-300 USD per night

- **Address:** 77 Rue des Remparts, Québec, QC G1R 5L1, Canada

- **Phone:** +1 418-694-1616

- **Facilities:** Simple and comfortable rooms, museum, spa, restaurant with healthy cuisine, yoga and meditation classes, historical exhibits.

- **About:** A unique and serene retreat offering a holistic experience with a focus on wellness and history.

14. Monsieur Jean - Hôtel Particulier: This intimate boutique hotel offers a personalized experience with just 18 uniquely designed rooms and suites.

- **Price Range:** $250-400+ USD per night

- **Address:** 44 Rue Saint-Louis, Québec, QC G1R 3Z3, Canada

- **Phone:** +1 418-570-4444

- **Facilities:** Luxurious rooms and suites with unique designs, free Wi-Fi, concierge service, breakfast included.

- **About:** A personalized and intimate experience in a beautifully restored historic building.

15. Hôtel Le Germain Québec: Modern hotel with stylish décor, comfortable rooms, and a prime location near the Parliament Building.

- **Price Range:** $200-350+ USD per night

- **Address:** 126 Rue Saint-Pierre, Québec, QC G1K 4A8, Canada

- **Phone:** +1 418-640-4000

- **Facilities:** Modern rooms and suites, free Wi-Fi, fitness center, on-site restaurant, bar, pet-friendly.

- **About:** A contemporary and comfortable option with a central location and a focus on personalized service.

Charming Bed & Breakfasts:

16. Gîte B&B du Vieux-Port: Cozy bed and breakfast in the Old Port with charming rooms, antique furniture, and a delicious homemade breakfast with river views.

- **Price Range:** $100-180 USD per night

- **Address:** 51 Rue Saint-Paul, Québec, QC G1K 3V8, Canada

- **Phone:** +1 418-692-1323

- **Facilities:** Comfortable rooms, free Wi-Fi, breakfast included, terrace with river views.

- **About:** Offers a warm and welcoming atmosphere with personalized service and a focus on local charm.

17. Auberge Place d'Armes: Charming inn in the Old City with individually decorated rooms, a cozy fireplace in the common area, and a delightful breakfast served in a charming dining room.

- **Price Range:** $120-200 USD per night

- **Address:** 10 Rue Sainte-Anne, Québec, QC G1R 3X2, Canada

- **Phone:** +1 418-692-1749

- **Facilities:** Cozy rooms, free Wi-Fi, breakfast included, fireplace in common area.

- **About:** A charming and historic inn with a central location and personalized service.

18. Au coeur du Vieux-Québec: Cozy B&B located in a historic building with comfortable rooms and a warm, welcoming atmosphere, perfect for a romantic getaway.

- **Price Range:** $110-190 USD per night

- **Address:** 23 Rue Sainte-Famille, Québec, QC G1R 4J9, Canada

- **Phone:** +1 418-692-1573

- **Facilities:** Comfortable rooms, free Wi-Fi, breakfast included.

- **About:** A charming and intimate B&B with a focus on personalized service and a quiet atmosphere.

19. La Marquise de Bassano: Elegant B&B housed in a 19th-century mansion, offering luxurious rooms with antique furnishings and a gourmet breakfast served in a beautiful dining room.

- **Price Range:** $180-300+ USD per night

- **Address:** 4 Rue des Grisons, Québec, QC G1R 4B3, Canada

- **Phone:** +1 418-694-1727

- **Facilities:** Luxurious rooms, free Wi-Fi, gourmet breakfast included, beautiful garden.

- **About:** A luxurious and romantic retreat with a focus on elegance and comfort.

20. Maison du Fort: Charming B&B in a historic building with cozy rooms, a beautiful garden, and a hearty breakfast featuring local ingredients.

- **Price Range:** $120-200 USD per night

- **Address:** 1 Rue des Carrières, Québec, QC G1R 4P5, Canada

- **Phone:** +1 418-692-1533

- **Facilities:** Comfortable rooms, free Wi-Fi, breakfast included, beautiful garden.

- **About:** A warm and inviting B&B with a focus on local charm and hospitality.

11. ACTIVITIES & EXPERIENCES

Outdoor Adventures: Get Active in Québec City

Québec City is a playground for outdoor enthusiasts, offering a variety of activities for all ages and skill levels. Whether you prefer hiking through lush forests, biking along scenic routes, or paddling on the majestic St. Lawrence River, there's definitely something for everyone to enjoy.

Outdoor Adventures:

- **Hiking:** Explore the Plains of Abraham's network of trails, offering stunning views of the city and the river. For a more challenging hike, venture to the nearby Mont-Sainte-Anne, a popular ski resort that transforms into a hiker's paradise in the warmer months.

- **Biking:** Discover Québec City on two wheels! The city boasts numerous bike paths, including the scenic Samuel-De Champlain Promenade along the St. Lawrence River. If you're feeling adventurous, rent a bike and explore the surrounding countryside, where you'll find charming villages, rolling hills, and picturesque vineyards.

- **Kayaking or Canoeing:** Get a unique perspective of Québec City by paddling along the St. Lawrence River. Several rental companies offer guided tours or independent rentals, allowing you to explore at your own pace.

Other Outdoor Activities:

- **Parc national de la Jacques-Cartier:** Just a short drive from Québec City, this park offers a plethora of outdoor activities, including hiking, fishing, canoeing, and wildlife watching.

- **Parc de la Chute-Montmorency:** This park is not only home to the magnificent Montmorency Falls but also offers hiking trails, a via ferrata (protected climbing route), and a zipline adventure.

- **Canyon Sainte-Anne:** Located about 40 kilometers (25 miles) east of Québec City, this impressive canyon features waterfalls, suspension bridges, and hiking trails for all levels.

No matter what your preferred activity, Québec City and its surrounding areas provide endless opportunities to get active and enjoy the great outdoors.

Experiencing Local Culture (Museums, Art Galleries, Shows

Québec City's rich cultural heritage is on full display in its many museums, art galleries, and performance venues.

Museums:

- **Musée de la Civilisation:** This world-class museum explores Québec's diverse history and culture through interactive exhibits, captivating artifacts, and thought-provoking displays. Immerse yourself in the stories of the province's people, from Indigenous communities to French settlers, and gain a deeper understanding of the forces that have shaped this unique region.

- **Musée national des beaux-arts du Québec (MNBAQ):** Art lovers will be captivated by this renowned museum, which houses a vast collection of Québec and Canadian art. Explore the galleries showcasing paintings, sculptures, installations, and other works by both established and emerging artists. Don't miss the stunning sculpture garden, a peaceful oasis offering breathtaking views of the St. Lawrence River.

Art Galleries and Cultural Centers:

- **Galerie 3:** This contemporary art gallery showcases the work of local and international artists, with a focus on emerging talent and innovative mediums.

- **Engramme - centre de production en estampe et diffusion en art actuel:** This printmaking center and art gallery offers a unique opportunity to see artists at work and explore contemporary printmaking techniques.

- **Maison de la littérature:** Housed in a former church, this literary center hosts readings, workshops, and exhibitions related to literature and writing. It's a haven for book lovers and a place to discover new voices in Québec's literary scene.

Shows and Performances:

- **Grand Théâtre de Québec:** This impressive performing arts complex hosts a wide range of shows, including operas, ballets, symphony concerts, and plays.

- **Palais Montcalm:** Located in the heart of Old Québec, this historic theater presents a diverse program of classical music, jazz, dance, and other performances.

- **Le Diamant:** This modern theater is home to a variety of productions, including contemporary plays, musicals, and experimental performances.

- **Théâtre Capitole:** This ornate theater, originally built as a cinema, now hosts concerts, musicals, and other events.

Tip: Check the websites or social media pages of these venues to see what's playing during your visit. You might be surprised by the variety and quality of the shows available!

Family Fun (Parks, Zoos, Playgrounds)

Québec City isn't just about historic charm; it's also a playground for families, offering a variety of outdoor spaces and attractions that cater to children of all ages.

Parks & Playgrounds:

- **Parc de la Chute-Montmorency:** While known for its majestic waterfall, this park also boasts vast green spaces, perfect for picnicking, playing frisbee, or simply running around. Kids will love exploring the trails and discovering hidden waterfalls.

- **Parc Jeanne-Mance:** Located in the heart of the Plains of Abraham, this park features a large playground with swings, slides, and climbing structures. It's also home to a wading pool and a splash pad, perfect for cooling off on hot summer days.

- **Parc Victoria:** Situated in the Saint-Roch neighborhood, this park offers a playground, a skating rink in the winter, and a charming carousel that's sure to delight little ones.

- **Parc du Bois-de-Coulonge:** This hidden gem features beautiful gardens, walking trails, and a large playground with a variety of equipment for different ages. It's a peaceful oasis where families can relax and enjoy nature.

Aquarium du Québec:

No family trip to Québec City would be complete without a visit to the Aquarium du Québec. This impressive aquarium is home to over 10,000 marine animals, from playful seals and walruses to colorful fish and fascinating invertebrates. Kids will love watching the underwater shows, exploring the touch tanks, and learning about the importance of marine conservation.

Playgrounds & Outdoor Spaces:

In addition to the larger parks, you'll find numerous playgrounds and outdoor spaces scattered throughout the city, perfect for a quick stop to let the kids burn off some energy. Look for these signs of fun in neighborhoods like Limoilou, Saint-Sauveur, and Sillery.

Tip: Pack a picnic lunch and head to one of these parks for a fun and affordable family outing! You can enjoy the fresh air, scenic views, and let the kids play to their hearts' content.

Québec City offers a wealth of opportunities for families to create lasting memories. With its diverse range of outdoor spaces and kid-friendly attractions, it's a destination where everyone can have fun and make the most of their vacation.

Seasonal Activities (Winter Carnivals, Summer Festivals)

The City comes alive with vibrant festivals and events throughout the year, celebrating its rich culture, history, and natural beauty.

Winter Wonderland: Québec Winter Carnival (Carnaval de Québec)

From late January to mid-February, Québec City transforms into a magical winter wonderland during the Carnaval de Québec. This world-renowned festival is a true celebration of winter, featuring:

- **Bonhomme Carnaval:** The beloved snowman mascot of the carnival, Bonhomme is a symbol of joy and fun for all ages. You'll see him everywhere during the festivities, from parades to ice palaces.

- **Ice Palace:** A magnificent structure made entirely of ice, the Ice Palace is a marvel of architecture and engineering. It's a popular spot for photos and a must-see for any visitor.

- **Ice Canoe Race:** Witness the thrilling spectacle of teams racing across the frozen St. Lawrence River in traditional ice canoes.

- **Night Parades:** Bundle up and enjoy the festive night parades, featuring illuminated floats, costumed characters, and lively music.

- **Snow Sculptures:** Admire the intricate and imaginative snow sculptures created by talented artists from around the world.

- **Outdoor Activities:** Embrace the winter spirit with activities like snow tubing, ice skating, and sleigh rides.

Summertime Fun: Festival d'été de Québec (FEQ)

As the snow melts and the days grow longer, Québec City bursts into life with the Festival d'été de Québec (FEQ), one of North America's largest music festivals. This 11-day extravaganza features a diverse lineup of international and local artists performing on multiple stages throughout the city.

- **Outdoor Concerts:** Rock out to your favorite bands or discover new musical talent at the outdoor concerts held in the Plains of Abraham and other iconic locations.

- **Street Performances:** Stroll through the streets and enjoy spontaneous performances by musicians, dancers, and street artists.

- **Cultural Events:** FEQ isn't just about music; it's a celebration of Québec's vibrant culture. Attend art exhibitions, film screenings, and other cultural events that take place throughout the festival.

Other Seasonal Events:

- **New France Festival (Les Fêtes de la Nouvelle-France):** Step back in time to the 17th and 18th centuries during this historical festival, which celebrates Québec City's French colonial roots with re-enactments, period costumes, and traditional music and dance.

- **Wendake International Pow Wow:** This annual event in the nearby Wendake Huron Village celebrates

Indigenous culture with traditional dance, music, food, and crafts.

No matter when you visit, Québec City offers a festive atmosphere and a chance to experience the city's unique cultural traditions.

12. PRACTICAL TIPS

Local Customs & Etiquette

Québec City is known for its friendly and welcoming atmosphere, but understanding a few local customs will help you blend in and show respect for the local culture:

Greetings:

- **Bonjour/Bonsoir:** It's customary to greet people with a warm "bonjour" (good day) or "bonsoir" (good evening) when entering a shop, restaurant, or other establishment. Likewise, say "au revoir" (goodbye) when leaving. This simple gesture goes a long way in showing politeness and respect.

Courtesy and Respect:

- **Holding the Door:** It's considered polite to hold the door open for the person behind you, whether it's at a store, restaurant, or even on the street.

- **Offering Your Seat:** On public transportation, it's customary to offer your seat to elderly people, pregnant women, or those with disabilities.

Tipping:

Tipping is a common practice in Québec City, and it's expected for good service in various situations:

- **Restaurants:** A standard tip of 15-20% of the pre-tax bill is customary for good service. If service was exceptional, you can tip more.

- **Taxis:** Round up the fare to the nearest dollar or add a few dollars as a tip.

- **Hotels:** Tip $1-2 CAD per bag for bellhops and $2-5 CAD per day for housekeeping staff.

Additional Tips:

- **Personal Space:** Québécois generally maintain a comfortable distance when conversing with others. Avoid standing too close or touching someone unnecessarily.

- **Punctuality:** Being on time is important, whether it's for a meeting, social gathering, or tour.

- **Smoking:** Smoking is prohibited in most indoor public places and within a certain distance of doorways.

By observing these local customs and etiquette, you'll ensure a positive and respectful interaction with the people of Québec City, enhancing your overall travel experience.

Useful French Phrases

Although English is commonly used in tourist spots, picking up a few basic French phrases will enrich your trip and demonstrate appreciation for the local culture. Here are some key phrases to get you started:

Greetings & Essentials:

1. Bonjour/Bonsoir: Hello/Good evening

2. Salut: Hi (informal)

3. Au revoir: Goodbye

4. À bientôt: See you soon

5. Bonne journée: Have a good day

6. Bonne soirée: Have a good evening

7. Merci: Thank you

8. Merci beaucoup: Thank you very much

9. De rien: You're welcome

10. S'il vous plaît: Please

11. Excusez-moi: Excuse me

12. Pardon: Sorry

13. Oui: Yes

14. Non: No

15. D'accord: Okay

Questions & Directions:

1. Parlez-vous anglais?: Do you speak English?

2. Où sont les toilettes?: Where are the restrooms?

3. Pouvez-vous parler plus lentement?: Can you speak more slowly?

4. Pouvez-vous répéter?: Can you repeat?

5. Où est...?: Where is...?

6. Comment puis-je aller à...?: How can I get to...?

7. Combien ça coûte?: How much does it cost?

8. Quelle heure est-il?: What time is it?

9. Pouvez-vous m'aider?: Can you help me?

10. Je suis perdu(e): I'm lost

11. Y a-t-il un bus pour...?: Is there a bus to...?

12.   Où puis-je trouver un taxi?: Where can I find a taxi?

13.   C'est loin?: Is it far?

14.   Je cherche une pharmacie: I'm looking for a pharmacy

15.   Y a-t-il un guichet automatique près d'ici?: Is there an ATM nearby?

Dining & Shopping:

1. Je voudrais... (un café, une bière, etc.): I would like... (a coffee, a beer, etc.)

2. Un café, s'il vous plaît: A coffee, please

3. Je prends... (le plat du jour, la soupe, etc.): I'll take... (the dish of the day, the soup, etc.)

4. L'addition, s'il vous plaît: The bill, please

5. Je cherche... (un souvenir, des vêtements, etc.): I'm looking for... (a souvenir, clothes, etc.)

6. Quelle taille faites-vous?: What size are you? (for clothing)

7. Est-ce que je peux essayer?: Can I try it on?

8. C'est trop cher: It's too expensive

9. Avez-vous quelque chose de moins cher?: Do you have something less expensive?

10. Je vais prendre celui-ci/celle-ci: I'll take this one

11. Merci, je regarde seulement: Thank you, I'm just looking

12. C'est tout?: Is that all?

13. C'est délicieux!: It's delicious!

14. Avez-vous une table pour deux?: Do you have a table for two?

15. Je suis végétarien(ne)/végan(e): I'm vegetarian/vegan

Remember:

- Practice the pronunciation of these phrases before your trip.

- Don't be afraid to make mistakes – the locals appreciate your effort to communicate in their language.

- Use gestures and a smile to help get your message across.

These phrases will help you navigate various situations and interact with locals confidently during your Québec City adventure!

Things to Avoid (Common Tourist Traps or Mistakes)

While Québec City is a welcoming and safe destination, it's always wise to be aware of potential tourist traps and common mistakes. Here are 20 things to avoid ensuring a smooth and enjoyable trip:

1. **Overpriced Souvenirs:** Don't buy souvenirs at the first shop you see in touristy areas like Rue du Petit-Champlain. Explore side streets and local markets for more unique and affordable options.

2. **Assuming Everyone Speaks English:** While many locals speak English, especially in the tourism industry, it's polite to learn a few basic French phrases and not assume fluency.

3. **Skipping the Local Cuisine:** Don't limit yourself to familiar international chains. Québec City has a vibrant culinary scene with unique dishes and flavors to discover.

4. **Only Staying in the Old Town:** While charming, the Old Town is just one part of Québec City. Explore other neighborhoods like Saint-Roch and Saint-Jean-Baptiste for a more authentic experience.

5. **Ignoring the Weather:** Québec City's weather can be unpredictable, so check the forecast and pack accordingly. Don't get caught unprepared for rain, snow, or heatwaves.

6. **Not Booking Accommodations in Advance:** Québec City is a popular destination, especially during peak seasons. Book your accommodations early to avoid disappointment and higher prices.

7. **Overpacking:** Cobblestone streets and hills can make lugging heavy suitcases a challenge. Pack light and consider bringing a backpack or rolling suitcase with sturdy wheels.

8. **Not Trying Poutine:** This iconic Québécois dish is a must-try, even if you're not a fan of gravy and cheese curds. You might be surprised!

9. **Missing the Changing of the Guard Ceremony:** This colorful and historic spectacle at the Citadelle is a free and entertaining way to experience Québec City's military heritage.

10.   **Neglecting the Local Culture:** Québec City has a unique culture and history. Learn a few French phrases, try local dishes, and explore neighborhoods beyond the tourist hotspots.

11.   **Underestimating the Cost of Taxis:** Taxis can be expensive, especially if you're traveling long distances. Consider using public transportation or ride-sharing services for a more budget-friendly option.

12.   **Falling for Tourist Traps:** Beware of overly friendly individuals offering unsolicited advice or trying to lure you into overpriced shops or restaurants. Trust your instincts and do your research.

13.   **Being Loud and Disrespectful:** Québécois are generally polite and reserved. Avoid being overly loud in public places or disrespecting local customs and traditions.

14.   **Not Tipping:** Tipping is customary in Québec City for good service in restaurants, bars, and taxis. Be sure to factor this into your budget.

15.   **Only Visiting in the Summer:** Québec City is beautiful in all seasons. Consider visiting during the

shoulder seasons (spring or fall) for fewer crowds and lower prices.

16.   **Not Trying Maple Syrup:** Québec is famous for its maple syrup. Sample it on pancakes, waffles, or even in cocktails for a true taste of the region.

17.   **Skipping the Local Markets:** Québec City's markets, like the Marché du Vieux-Port, offer a vibrant atmosphere and a chance to sample local produce, crafts, and culinary delights.

18.   **Not Exploring Beyond the City Walls:** Venture beyond the Old Town to discover other charming neighborhoods like Saint-Roch and Saint-Jean-Baptiste, each with its own unique character and attractions.

19.   **Relying Solely on Credit Cards:** While credit cards are widely accepted, it's wise to carry some cash for smaller shops, markets, and tipping.

20.   **Not Taking Time to Relax:** While there's much to see and do in Québec City, don't forget to slow down and savor the moment. Relax in a park, sip a coffee in a cozy café, or simply wander the streets and soak up the atmosphere.

By avoiding these common pitfalls, you'll be well on your way to experiencing the best that Québec City has to offer!

Staying Safe & Connected (Emergency Contacts)

Québec City is a safe and welcoming destination, but it's always wise to be prepared for any situation. Here are some tips to help you stay safe and connected during your trip:

Emergency Contacts:

In case of emergency, dial 911 for police, ambulance, or fire services. This number is free to call from any phone, including public payphones.

Additional Emergency Numbers:

- **Non-emergency Police:** 418-641-AGIR (2447)
- **Info-Santé:** 811 (for non-urgent health advice)

Offline Map App:

To avoid getting lost or relying on expensive data roaming, download a reliable offline map app for your smartphone. This will allow you to navigate the city even without an internet connection. Some popular options include:

- **Maps.me:** This app offers detailed maps of Québec City and other destinations around the world. You can download maps for offline use and even save specific locations for easy access.

- **Google Maps:** You can download maps of specific areas in Google Maps for offline use. This is a convenient option if you already use Google Maps for navigation.

Staying Connected:

- **Local SIM Card:** If you plan on using your phone frequently for calls, texts, or data, consider purchasing a local SIM card from a Canadian mobile provider. This provides you with a local phone number and access to budget-friendly data plans.

- **Portable Wi-Fi Hotspot:** If you have multiple devices or prefer to use your own SIM card, a portable Wi-Fi hotspot can be a great option. You can rent one from a travel agency or purchase one before your trip.

- **Free Wi-Fi:** Many cafes, restaurants, and hotels in Québec City offer free Wi-Fi for guests. Utilize these hotspots to remain online without consuming your data.

Additional Safety Tips:

- **Be aware of your surroundings:** Pay attention to your belongings and be cautious in crowded areas, especially at night.

- **Let someone know your plans:** Inform a friend or family member of your itinerary and expected return time.

- **Carry a copy of your passport and other important documents:** This will be helpful in case of loss or theft.

- **Learn a few basic French phrases:** Even if you speak English, learning a few basic French phrases will help you communicate with locals and navigate the city.

By following these tips, you can ensure a safe and enjoyable trip to Québec City. Remember, the most important thing is to be prepared, stay informed, and use common sense.

Languages Spoken in Québec

Languages Spoken in Québec City: A Bilingual Experience

While exploring Québec City, you'll quickly notice that French is the predominant language. It's the official language of the province and the primary language spoken in everyday life, from street signs and menus to conversations among locals.

Don't worry if you don't speak French fluently, as English is also widely spoken and understood, particularly in tourist areas, hotels, restaurants, and shops. Most people working in the tourism industry are bilingual and happy to assist you in English.

However, venturing beyond the main tourist hubs, you might encounter situations where English isn't as common. Embrace this opportunity to immerse yourself in the French language and culture by learning a few basic phrases.

Here's why it's worth learning a few words of French:

- **Show Respect:** Making an effort to speak French shows respect for the local culture and demonstrates your willingness to engage with the community.

- **Enhance Your Experience:** Even a few simple phrases can open doors to deeper connections with locals and enrich your travel experience.

- **Navigate with Ease:** Knowing basic phrases for asking directions or ordering food can make your trip smoother and more enjoyable.

While you'll likely get by with English, learning a bit of French will go a long way in showing appreciation for Québec City's unique culture and making your trip even more memorable. Consider it a fun challenge and an opportunity to broaden your horizons!

I've provided a list of useful French phrases earlier in this guide (page 128) to get you started. Don't hesitate to use them and practice your pronunciation. You'll be amazed at how fast you can learn the essentials!

SUGGESTED ITINENARY

Now that you've explored the best of Québec City's attractions, flavors, and experiences, it's time to start crafting your own unique adventure. To help you get started, we've put together a few sample itineraries that cater to different interests and lengths of stay. These are just suggestions, of course – feel free to mix and match activities based on your preferences and the time you have available.

Short & Sweet (3 Days):

- **Day 1:** discover the historic charm of Old Québec. Visit the iconic landmarks like Château Frontenac and the Citadelle, stroll along Rue du Petit-Champlain, and savor a delicious meal at a traditional restaurant.

- **Day 2:** Discover the natural beauty of Montmorency Falls, either by taking a scenic bus ride or embarking on a hiking adventure. In the afternoon, explore the unique cultural attractions of Wendake Huron Village.

- **Day 3 (Optional):** If you have an extra day, take a ferry to Lévis for stunning views of Québec City or embark on a day trip to Île d'Orléans to experience its charming villages and local flavors.

A Week in Québec City:

- **Days 1-2:** Follow the Short & Sweet itinerary above to get acquainted with the city's highlights.

- **Day 3:** Explore Québec City's vibrant arts scene. Visit the Musée de la Civilisation or the Musée national des beaux-arts du Québec, explore art galleries in Saint-Roch, or catch a show at the Grand Théâtre de Québec.

- **Day 4:** Venture beyond the city walls and explore the surrounding areas. Take a scenic drive or bike ride along the St. Lawrence River, visit the Jacques-Cartier

National Park for hiking and nature immersion, or try your hand at ice canoeing (in winter).

- **Day 5:** Indulge in a culinary adventure. Sample local specialties at the Marché du Vieux-Port, try poutine at a traditional restaurant, or savor a gourmet meal at a fine-dining establishment. Don't forget to explore the charming shops and boutiques in Old Québec and Saint-Roch.

- **Day 6:** Relax and recharge. Stroll through the peaceful Parc du Bois-de-Coulonge, unwind at a local spa, or simply soak up the atmosphere at a sidewalk café.

- **Day 7:** Choose your own adventure! Visit a sugar shack for a taste of local tradition, attend a hockey game to experience Québec City's passion for the sport, or simply wander the streets and discover your own hidden gems.

Remember: *These are just suggestions! Feel free to mix and match activities based on your interests and time constraints. And don't forget to leave some room for spontaneity – some of the best travel experiences happen when you wander off the beaten path and follow your curiosity.*

CONCLUSION

As you turn the final page of this pocket guide, we hope you're brimming with excitement and anticipation for your Québec City adventure. This enchanting city, with its blend of European charm, rich history, and vibrant culture, is a destination that promises to delight and surprise you at every turn.

Whether you're strolling through the cobblestone streets of Old Québec, savoring the flavors of poutine, cheering on the Remparts at a hockey game, or venturing off the beaten path to discover hidden gems, we hope this guide has equipped you with the knowledge and inspiration to make the most of your visit.

Québec City is a city that welcomes you with open arms, a place where you can create lasting memories and connect with a unique and vibrant culture. So pack your bags, practice your "bonjours," and get ready for an unforgettable journey!

As the Québécois say, "Bon voyage!" We are eager to learn about your experiences in Québec City.

Happy exploring!

As a bonus, we've included a few word search puzzles to add a touch of fun and challenge to your journey.

Word Search Fun

Take a break from exploring and challenge yourself with these word searches! They're a fun way to test your knowledge of the city's landmarks, neighborhoods, cuisine, and more. So, grab a pen and see how many words you can find!

Answers?

Want to check your answers to the word search puzzles? Simply scan the QR code below to access the solutions for free!

Has this book been helpful to you in any way? If so, we'd be delighted if you could share your experience with other travelers by leaving a review on Amazon. Your feedback helps us improve and lets others discover the magic of Québec City too!

Culture

N	E	M	Y	U	R	C	A	E	S	A	R	T	T
R	R	T	H	T	T	R	R	R	A	T	O	L	R
D	T	P	C	R	I	T	U	A	L	R	Y	S	A
U	A	A	N	A	T	S	O	M	F	A	N	L	E
H	E	R	E	A	A	A	T	U	T	T	C	N	E
M	H	A	R	A	W	C	I	I	R	O	T	C	S
M	T	D	F	R	U	M	D	A	N	C	E	E	H
C	R	E	O	S	R	O	U	A	U	A	S	T	O
H	A	P	T	E	D	P	S	R	F	O	S	E	W
A	T	O	L	A	E	E	R	Y	A	A	L	M	C
N	M	A	F	A	H	R	P	R	N	L	R	U	A
T	A	A	T	S	Y	A	T	O	A	H	C	S	Y
P	E	P	D	Y	C	H	I	T	A	R	T	I	C
Y	A	H	P	T	E	E	T	S	T	T	U	C	R

Word list:

MUSIC
PLAY
THEATRE
CRAFT
CUSTOM
ART
TOUR
MURAL
FRENCH
STORY
OPERA
STYLE
DANCE
CHANT
RITUAL
PARADE
SHOW

Tourism

E	T	U	O	R	E	H	K	L	V	R	N	I	L
S	R	I	N	E	V	U	O	S	E	R	O	N	I
V	L	O	U	A	R	S	P	U	W	E	W	R	D
E	O	E	L	T	R	A	I	L	D	R	T	U	O
O	E	T	V	S	T	R	O	L	L	T	T	O	C
T	R	T	T	A	U	W	T	D	R	R	H	J	V
R	N	R	E	E	R	T	H	E	R	U	W	O	U
R	W	I	K	O	I	T	J	J	O	O	A	S	O
S	U	P	C	G	U	I	D	E	V	T	L	A	L
I	E	V	I	U	N	V	T	O	T	L	K	T	O
G	L	I	T	R	K	E	W	E	E	I	N	T	J
H	S	S	L	W	A	N	D	E	R	I	O	T	E
T	E	I	H	O	T	E	L	E	I	H	O	T	T
O	P	T	U	W	R	T	U	U	P	V	E	A	O

WALK
TICKET
VIEW
TRAVEL
SOUVENIRS
GUIDE
SIGHT
ROUTE
TRAIL
PHOTO
SOJOURN
WANDER
TOUR
HOTEL
STROLL
VISIT
TRIP

Activities

K	L	W	I	S	I	H	V	E	S	L	L	C	L
S	E	T	A	K	C	R	I	K	D	P	R	I	H
I	I	S	O	T	S	D	S	I	A	A	S	R	E
E	K	K	A	A	C	C	I	H	D	K	T	E	K
O	L	W	S	E	A	R	T	K	A	R	K	R	E
T	L	S	B	C	E	T	P	W	I	T	A	O	R
K	O	R	M	B	K	T	D	D	R	S	G	L	U
A	R	E	I	L	A	A	R	R	G	K	T	P	O
Y	T	D	L	S	R	S	L	E	D	N	H	X	T
A	S	E	C	K	W	A	N	D	E	R	G	E	K
K	R	P	I	A	T	K	U	O	K	D	U	X	C
C	A	R	T	T	B	I	K	I	N	G	H	I	H
I	I	E	S	E	S	E	S	I	U	R	C	S	G
P	A	D	D	L	E	R	L	E	I	E	K	A	N

SLED
VISIT
WANDER
SKATE
WATCH
TOUR
CLIMB
HIKE
STROLL
KAYAK
BIKING
PADDLE
SKI
EXPLORE
CRUISE

food

F	G	A	A	C	S	C	S	P	A	S	T	R	Y
B	R	P	U	T	H	U	Y	R	B	E	A	N	S
R	S	U	E	P	R	E	G	O	E	A	R	R	E
F	R	L	E	M	O	N	E	A	G	T	U	T	P
O	C	R	E	T	O	N	S	S	R	U	A	E	A
B	A	C	O	N	E	T	P	F	E	B	R	W	S
T	C	C	P	S	E	P	A	R	G	M	T	T	T
I	O	A	O	A	E	B	O	T	U	H	I	S	A
U	F	A	U	L	E	E	C	F	D	U	O	P	C
C	F	T	T	A	E	G	F	P	R	D	T	N	S
S	E	E	I	D	O	I	N	F	T	E	R	U	I
I	E	C	N	A	N	B	R	E	A	D	P	U	R
B	S	T	E	A	K	C	O	O	K	I	E	W	O
E	I	A	P	P	L	E	R	I	E	K	E	I	P

COFFEE
MUFFIN
BREAD
PASTRY
SIROP
STEAK
FRUITS
CRETONS
SUGAR
POUTINE
GRAPES
BACON
BEANS
APPLE
CHEESE
PASTA
BISCUIT
LEMON
SALAD
YOGURT
COOKIE
WATER

NOTES

Made in the USA
Las Vegas, NV
19 December 2024

15010661R00085